What Our Gurus Taught Us

What Our Gurus Taught Us

Stories from Hinduism's Great Teachers

Renuka Narayanan

JUGGERNAUT BOOKS
KS House, 118 Shahpur Jat, New Delhi 110049, India

First published as *Hindu Fables from the Vedas to Vivekananda*
by Juggernaut Books 2017
This edition published 2020

10 9 8 7 6 5 4 3 2

ISBN 9789353450960

Typeset in Adobe Caslon Pro by R. Ajith Kumar, New Delhi

Printed at Thomson Press India Ltd

Contents

1

What the Thunder Says

In one of the oldest of old Indian books, the main 'action' in the story is the longing to know. Its characters yearn for knowledge about the universe and its ways, and attempt to identify and state mankind's place in the scheme of things through discussing a moral and spiritual code. The name of the book means 'The Teachings of the Great Wilderness' and, among other topics, it speculates on the causes of creation. It argues that there was nothing in the beginning, but beyond the matter and energy that now exist there is a Super-Consciousness or Super-Self or 'Supersoul' at work. This book is the *Brihad Aranyaka Upanishad*, a collection of Sanskrit parables, pensées, hymns and philosophical debates, in six sections. This key book in Hindu theology is believed to have been authored around 700 BCE by the ancient lawgiver Rishi Yajnavalkya, part-author of the holy book *Yajur Veda*. In the fifth section of the *Brihad Aranyaka Upanishad*, Yajnavalkya teaches his students the nature of human duty through the story 'What the Thunder Says'.

Brahma the Creator, hailed as Prajapati, the All-Father, had created three races – the celestials, the humans and the titans, called deva, manushya and asura in Sanskrit. They were made to respectively inhabit the three realms of the universe – the celestial world called Swarg, the earth in the middle called Prithvi and the netherworld called Patal.

Proud to be born and eager to please, the three races meditated together before they went in a body to the All-Father and said, 'Please instruct us.'

The All-Father accepted their greetings and nodded pleasantly. He looked them over with a critical eye before saying anything.

The celestials were light, airy beings bathed in light. Their realm, which they had named Indralok or Indra's World after their leader Indra or Sakra, was a fair dominion through which they chased the lightning, played with the thunderclouds and rode the rain. They had everything they could possibly want. They were free from hunger, thirst, pain and perspiration. The flower garlands they wore were ever-fresh and their feet did not touch the ground. They had no need to work or toil for anything and they would never grow old and die. There was music and dance in their realm and golden goblets of mead. They were the Immortals to whom the ones below had to offer sacrifice to obtain their favour and cooperation.

The All-Father nodded slightly as he noticed that the devas, particularly their leader Indra, had the beginnings of a crafty, libidinous look about the eye. They had plunged whole-heartedly into enjoyment and wore the raffish air of rakes.

He said to the celestials, 'This is my instruction to you. *Da.*' He said but that one word, da.

'Have you understood what I said?' he asked.

'Yes, we understand, All-Father.'

'Well done. Then follow that teaching.'

He looked next at the human beings.

The earthlings were an interdependent race, much weaker than the celestials. Their realm, the earth, was full of danger. They were exposed to the fury of the five elements and the shiftings and heavings of their physical terrain. Mountains rolled great boulders down on them, and mighty rivers broke their banks and washed them away with their dwellings of wattle and daub, thatch, wood and stone. Wolves and tigers tore them apart and tiny insects bit their skin, making them itch and scratch in pain. Sickness, old age and death claimed each one of them – no earthling could escape that. They had to think their way through every situation and work very hard to obtain the smallest ease or pleasure.

But though they were clearly interdependent, the earthlings had proved greedy. They wanted to grab everything and hoard everything, be it cows, land or the women of their species. They wanted more and more with every acquisition. They fought and killed each other over the smallest things. Their greed was not merely for material goods. They revelled in saying and doing unkind things merely for the spiteful pleasure of hurting each other.

The All-Father shook his head slightly. A fine mess, there. But what immense potential these puny earthlings possessed did they but know it. With observation and intuitive leaps of imagination followed by hard work, these disgraceful creatures had more creative power than even the celestials. They had the untapped ability to make new things that had never been seen before. And for all its perils and pitfalls, the earth they inhabited was so astoundingly beautiful that even the celestials secretly coveted it. 'I created them in my own image,' thought the

All-Father fondly. 'They are exasperating but very, very interesting. The devas have a certain…sameness. But my earthlings are wholly unpredictable except in being greedy, and it will be a pleasure to watch them grow and do things. I shall never be bored watching them try to find their better self.'

'Do you want instruction from me?' he asked them, putting on a stern face.

'Yes, All-Father, we do,' they chorused.

'Da,' he said again. 'Did you get my meaning?'

'Yes, All-Father, we did.'

'Very good! Now go forth and follow this instruction.'

It was the turn of the titans next, a lumbering, muscle-flexing lot, gigantic in size with strong, simple hearts. The asuras loved their realm Patal, which was beautiful with many treasures. Precious stones and minerals glowed and sparkled on their walls, silvery underground streams cooled the air and great iridescent serpents played with them and told them wonderful stories. But the asuras did not know their own strength and hurt those weaker than themselves. 'They are marvellous beings, capable of greatness. They can teach the devas and manushyas important things. But their fatal flaw is their temper. It makes them cruel,' thought the All-Father. 'However, theirs is an honourable race, too, created to keep the universe in balance. If only they were not so jealous of the airy, confident celestials and the puny but persistent earthlings.'

'Da,' he said to the titans and, like the others, they meekly answered, 'Yes, we have understood your meaning.'

'Go, then, and follow this instruction.'

And this was his meaning, understood differently by each according to their nature, taught Rishi Yajnavalkya.

The celestials understood da as damyata, meaning restraint. The All-Father had told them to exercise self-control on their pleasure-loving natures.

The earthlings understood da as datta, meaning 'Give, be generous,' which was the only way for an interdependent species to survive and flourish.

The titans understood da as dayadhvam, 'Be merciful,' which instructed them to curb their natural ferocity.

When the thunder rolls 'Da! Da! Da!' it echoes the voice of Prajapati, the All-Father, reminding the celestials, earthlings and titans of their eternal watchwords.

2

How the Butcher Taught the Brahmin

The *Vana Parva* or Book of the Forest is the longest section of the 'the world's longest epic', the *Mahabharata*. This was composed mostly by Veda Vyasa around 400 BCE and the *Vana Parva* is the third of the epic's eighteen sections. Though the *Vana Parva* is very long, with 21 subsections and 324 chapters, it is one of the most popular passages in Indian literature. It vividly describes the adventurous twelve-year stay of the Pandavas in the forest, the lessons they learn there and how the terrors and triumphs of the experience build their character. The parables in it are widely retold as independent stories in the major Indian languages and enacted in the traditional performing arts. In this story from the *Vana Parva* that sounds almost contemporary, Rishi Markandeya teaches Yudhishthir, the eldest Pandava prince, about the nature of dharma through the parable of the ascetic, the housewife and the butcher.

There was a very learned brahmin, Kausika by name, who devoted himself for many long years with utmost diligence to the study of the holy books. He sought out the best teachers he could access and was finally able to memorize and flawlessly recite the entire length of the Vedas. A full, proper parayanam or Vedic recitation required tremendous stamina for it took forty-five hours of non-stop chanting. The divine mantras produced so much heat in the body that, unless they had learned to cool their minds into the spiritually realized state of deep and absolute calm called amritsaras, or lake of nectar, many priests were prone to stomach ulcers and had to be dosed daily with day-old rice, buttermilk and ghee to save their stomach lining.

Kausika proved adept at both practising hard austerities and at Vedic chanting. One day, having stationed himself in the shade of a babul tree, he began to recite a portion of the Vedas. As he began, a sarus crane perched high above innocently let fall its droppings on his head. Angered by this 'disrespect', Kausika glared at the bird with such fury that the poor creature, unable to bear the blazing heat of his eyes, fell down dead.

Gratified at this evidence of his mental power, Kausika rinsed the bird droppings off his matted locks and sallied forth to beg his lunch from the townsfolk. He stopped outside a small but very trim, clean house and called out the alms-seeker's cry, '*Bhavati bhiksham dehi*', 'Whoever's there, give me alms.'

'Coming!' he heard a woman's voice call from within and waited expectantly, alms bowl at the ready. The minutes went by but nobody appeared bearing food. Kausika frowned, tutted in impatience and decided to wait just a little longer. After at least a quarter of an hour had passed, the lady of the house appeared at the door smiling, carrying a well-filled plate of food to serve in his alms bowl.

'Greetings, respected sage. I beg your pardon for having kept you waiting,' she said in a pleasant, contrite manner.

But Kausika snapped, 'Why did you not send me on my way? How dare you keep me waiting?' and glared furiously at her.

Nothing whatsoever happened to the housewife. Instead she looked at him thoughtfully. 'Did you think

I, too, was a bird?' she asked in an amused voice.

Kausika was taken aback. 'How did you know…' he said uncertainly.

'I knew, that's all. I really did not mean to keep you waiting, you know. My husband is an invalid. He called out for help just as I went to get your food. I had to settle him comfortably, fetch him some water, wait for him to drink it and make sure all was well with him before I could attend to you. Now do you understand? I see that you are very choleric,' she said.

'If that's the case…' muttered Kausika awkwardly, wonderstruck by this simple, unlettered housewife's omniscience.

She nodded wisely at him. 'I think you have a lot of questions, but I must get back to my duties. You have studied the Vedas and Upanishads at great length but the meaning of dharma eludes you still. If you will not take it amiss, my advice to you as a well-wisher is that you go to Mithila and seek out the wise butcher, Dharmavyadha. He will set your feet on the right path.' She smiled and, making polite obeisance, went away.

Proceeding to Mithila, Kausika wondered what he could possibly learn from a butcher. But his curiosity was fairly caught and to that great city of wise King Janaka he went and inquired after the butcher's whereabouts.

He was directed at once to Dharmavyadha's famous meat shop and as he approached, reluctance writ in every bone and muscle, the butcher glanced up and saw him. 'Welcome, O learned guest. The good housewife directed you to me, I see, after the bird was burned by your gaze. I believe she wanted you to discuss the nature of dharma with me. Please come in.'

Kausika was amazed. 'This is my second big surprise,' he told himself. The butcher took him home, made him welcome, seated him comfortably and asked how he could serve him. But Kausika had a question first. 'If you are such a virtuous person, why do you sell meat?' he asked.

'Learned guest, my family has sold meat for generations. There is nothing improper in this. I shrink, personally, from killing any creature, nor can I eat its flesh, just as a man may sell liquor but never touch a drop himself. However, this work, too, is part of society and so I fulfil my hereditary occupation to earn my living. It is not contrary to dharma or right conduct.

'However,' he added, 'though this is my job, I also devote a lot of time to looking after my old parents, who really need me now.'

'Very well, my good man. Please tell me what constitutes dharma.'

'Practising dharma is a combination of two kinds of

actions,' said the butcher musingly. 'One is to hold back on negative emotions like anger, greed, jealousy, malice, unrestrained lust and untruth. The other is to be proactive in the good things that build a good atmosphere and also make you feel well, things like politeness, kindness, compassion, giving gladly to the needy, being generally helpful and telling the truth – the virtues that hold society together.'

'Hmm. Yes, that does make sense. I see that you not only know dharma but practise it. I am amazed that you knew about me and so did the housewife, as if by divine insight. How did that happen?' asked Kausika.

'I am glad you recognize the spiritual attainment of that good lady. We don't know each other but she could tell you about me, and I knew that she had, through intuitive awareness. May I now give you some personal advice, if you will not be offended?' said Dharmavyadha.

'No, please do tell me,' said Kausika, wondering what lay in store.

'You went away to study the holy books to fulfil your ambitions, did you not – leaving your old parents to fend for themselves? They are lonely, sick and afraid and have wept themselves blind. It is good to have personal goals but we cannot abandon our personal duties either. I advise you to go home and look after them with loving kindness and a genuine desire to make them happy, not out of an arid sense of duty. If you can do that, the nature of dharma will light you up and you will never be angry or dejected or wish to hurt another creature. You can reclaim all that you have lost through active kindness and find true spiritual happiness. That is the right path for you,' said the butcher.

Kausika winced. He thought of his mother and father trying not to weep inauspiciously as he left home without a backward glance. Yet his mother had cooked his favourite food for his last meal at home and his father had fetched new upper and lower cloths for the dakshina or ceremonial present that Kausika would have to give the guru who accepted him as a student. Great waves of regret washed over Kausika, cleaning his soul of its arrogance. Well, if the Vedas taught you one thing, it was not to flinch from the truth, however unpleasant, he thought ruefully and looked at the butcher with real affection.

'Pure soul, you have convinced me that a clean heart and gratitude are the means to tell between right and wrong. I am vastly obliged to you. I shall take your excellent advice and look after my parents,' said Kausika and made his way home feeling light as cloud.

3

The Conch Bangles

One of the most sacred living texts that even occupies the place of the idol in the temple in some regions is the 'biography' of Sri Krishna, the beloved eighth avatar of Vishnu. It is formally known as the *Bhagvata Purana* or *Srimad Bhagvatam*, the holy story of god, or simply as the *Bhagvatam*, god's story. It was composed in Sanskrit by Veda Vyasa and, as other puranas do, it discusses a wide range of topics from cosmology, geography and myth to music, dance, yoga and culture. Its poetry is greatly admired and quoted across regions and communities. The *Bhagvatam* has between 16,000 and 18,000 verses depending on the edition. Its tenth chapter, with about 4000 verses, is the best-known and most widely studied. Incidentally, the *Bhagvatam* was the first purana to be translated into a European language, from a Tamil version to French, in 1788. In this parable from the *Bhagvatam*, Sri Krishna's earthly 'ancestor', King Yadu, is told by a young priest about how he learned to focus on his goal.

Lavanya was the daughter of a small cultivator who lived on the edge of a great forest of sal trees. He grew millet and vegetables and had but one cow, but it gave him, his wife and his daughter plenty of good, rich milk and his little fields were kind to him as were the weather gods.

As advised by wandering holy men on the right way to live, Lavanya's father divided his income into five shares. One share was for offerings to his ancestors, to repay the debt of having achieved human birth. One share was for the gods without whose favour nothing ever seemed to go well. One share was for guests and wayfarers, to be able to feed them properly, for that was a householder's prime duty. One share was for relatives, for as a son, brother, husband, father and uncle, a man had obligatory presents to give at ceremonies and festivals to affirm his relationships. The fifth share was to feed, clothe and shelter himself and his family.

A great many holy men went past their holding and stopped for a drink of water, a short rest and a simple dinner. They repaid the family by telling them wonderful stories by firelight when the day's work was done – stories of gods and titans, tricksters and heroes. Lavanya's natural intelligence was further energized by their tales.

One day, Lavanya's parents left for the weekly market three villages away, taking baskets of produce to sell. Lavanya soon finished her chores and sat down to weave a new basket of cane. But she had barely begun when four well-dressed people appeared in a bullock cart. They were her parents' age and announced that they had come with a proposal of marriage – for her.

'My son is a good, kind-hearted boy and we have many fields and cows. You will be well looked after and lack for nothing,' the prospective bridegroom's mother said, smiling. She wore a gold and coral necklace and gold bangles set with lucky hair from an elephant's tail. Her nose ring had pearls on it and her upper garment and lower garment were both of fine cotton and trimmed with borders of some rich weave.

'I'm sorry my parents are away at the weekly market, they'll be home only by sunset.' Lavanya blushed, feeling shy in this fine company.

'Oh, we'll wait here for them,' said the group cheerfully and looked about for a place in the shade. Lavanya scurried to drag out the string cots and spread grass mats on them for her guests to sit on. She fetched water for them, and a refreshing drink of jaggery juice in terracotta cups, and rounded up all the palmetto hand fans in her little home for the guests to use.

And then a terrible thought struck her.

'The evening meal!' she thought. 'We don't have enough husked rice to cook for everyone. I'd better husk more right away before I cut the vegetables.'

Excusing herself politely, Lavanya took out a good measure of unhusked paddy from the bin to the far end of the yard and began to pound it in the mortar with the long wooden pestle.

As she worked, the six conch bangles that she wore on either wrist began to clank merrily, 'Tak-taka-tak-tak! Tak-taka-tak-tak!'

'On, no!' thought Lavanya. 'What a noise these bangles make. How uncouth and impolite they will think me. And they'll wonder how poor I am that I wear such plain, simple bangles and not carved, pierced golden ones like they do.'

She broke four bangles on either wrist, leaving only two, and resumed husking the paddy.

But even those two clanked against each other as she worked, producing a childish, embarrassing sound as though a little boy or girl was running about in the yard playing with a wooden cart or clapper.

'This is no good. They will think I'm a real country bumpkin and hopelessly immature at that,' thought the intelligent maiden. 'However, I can't possibly go back in there completely bare-wristed, that is not considered proper in a girl. I know what! I'll break another bangle and leave on just the one.'

'I knew that intelligent maiden from previous visits to her home and that day I happened to come by but hung back and observed her actions quietly; and when I had the opportunity for a word, I asked her about it,' said the young priest to Yadu. 'From that incident, O King, I learned the value of solitude and concentration when an important personal task is at hand. Many people together will make a noise and may even break into a quarrel. They will ruin your enterprise. Even two people are likely to talk, argue and distract each other. That maiden's moves taught me to assess when to proceed alone on a life goal and why.'

4
Husbands and Wives

The *Markandeya Purana* is said to go as far back as c. 250 CE. 'Purana' means 'an old tale'; however, this book remains a living text with a powerful hold on popular belief. Chapters 81 to 93 of the *Markandeya Purana* form the famous *Chandi Paath* which celebrates Shakti, the sacred feminine. These verses are still recited every year during Durga Puja in October. Among the purana's 9000 verses is also found the terrifying tale of Raja Harishchandra, who sold his wife and son to keep his word. Harischandra was forced to tend a cremation ground at Varanasi or Kashi, the holiest of Hindu cities on the banks of the Ganga, the holiest Hindu river. Harishchandra Ghat in Kashi, where he is said to have done so, is still the most important and possibly the oldest continually used cremation ground in India; and Harishchandra's story, as the silent movie *Raja Harischandra*, was the first Indian film to be made, in 1912 by Dadasaheb Phalke, 'the father of Indian cinema'. In another story about relationships from this purana, Rishi Markandeya acquaints his disciple Kraustuki with the complicated give-and-take between husbands and wives.

Svarochh Manu, one of the ancestors of the human race, loved the company of women. Although he was permitted only one patrani or chief queen by custom, he made himself ridiculous by elevating three queens, Manorama, Vibhavari and Kalavati, to that position. His subjects sniggered openly at his lack of wit and there was worse to follow. One day when he was out jaunting on the river, a pair of ducks, mated for life in the way of their kind, swam past quacking in amusement. Svarochh could understand the speech of all living creatures and was greatly embarrassed when the female duck compared his personal life to hers and dismissed him scornfully as a pleasure-seeker incapable of loving anyone with commitment and sincerity. Another time, when out in the forest, he saw a doe frolicking amorously around a particularly handsome deer. The deer snubbed the doe with these harsh words, 'Pah! Be off. Do you think I'm Svarochh Manu to eagerly accept every female that throws herself at me?'

However, Svarochh Manu, despite his resolve to simplify his life, was unable to change his ways. After he passed away, he was remembered principally for his self-indulgence and lack of commitment, for exercising all kinds of 'rights' without a corresponding sense of duty.

This legacy of judgement was to haunt the Manu of the next epoch, King Uttama, who was happily married to a beautiful queen called Vahula. Though shy at heart, the queen was a practical person. She knew she had a tremendous public role to play and tried to cope. She participated with composure in all her queenly duties, be it in court or at the sacrificial fires. She administered her part of the palace sensibly, discouraged tale-bearing and petty quarrels and tried to give her household a good tone without being tiresomely pious. Her maids doted on her and the people spoke of her with respect.

Feeling secure in the esteem of those around her, Queen Vahula thanked the gods in her prayers. But soon, there followed a star-crossed phase. Perhaps the royal duties proved too much or familiarity had something to do with it, but Vahula no longer found her husband attractive or interesting. She began to withdraw subtly from him and with each passing week she withdrew more openly. The three pains according to Sankhya philosophy are Adhyatmika, those born of the mind and body, Adhidaivika or supernatural and Adhibhoutika, because of an incident, accident, mishap or calamity. All three were to fall together on this royal couple's heads.

The tension and the brooding silence between the king and queen grew and grew without a single conversation about it. One day at a public dinner with important merchants and foreign diplomats present, the wine flowed freely and the king had a bit too much. The queen did not drink but he offered her his goblet anyway in a noticeably public manner. The queen turned her head away with a frown and an awkward silence suddenly fell on the company. The king lost his temper and summoned a palace guard.

'Take the queen away and abandon her in the jungle,' he said. 'You are not permitted to question the right or wrong of my command.'

The guard bowed impassively to the queen and indicated that she should follow him, and Vahula swept away without a word, a proud smile on her face. 'She actually looked relieved to go' ran the gossip afterwards.

Soon after this catastrophe, a poor priest of the kingdom appeared in court to demand the king's help. Someone, possibly the neighbourhood rakshasa, or demon, had stolen his wife from their hut in the middle of the night.

'Describe her, we'll send out search parties,' said the king.

'She's not very pretty and not very amiable. In fact, she has a foul temper,' said the priest.

'What?' exclaimed King Uttama. 'It's easier to find you a pretty, new wife, you know.'

'Your Majesty,' said the priest reproachfully, 'my wife is my wife. It is my duty to keep her safe from the rest of the world, from my own family, and even from myself.'

'But you have no precise information about who took her away and where. Why should I exert myself fruitlessly chasing in all directions?' said the king.

'O Lord of the Earth, you take a sixth of our produce as your due and we, your subjects, can sleep fearlessly because you uphold the law,' said the priest.

Abashed, the king got up a stout hunting party and went to the forest inhabited by the demon. He soon found him, gawking at kingfishers diving into a forest pond, while the priest's wife sat inviolate nearby, placidly eating bel fruit.

'Hey, you!' roared King Uttama, at which the demon leaped to its feet and politely saluted him. 'I am your subject, too, Your Majesty, since I live in your kingdom,' it said meekly and awaited royal orders.

'Return this man's wife to him at once. Why did you kidnap her?' said the king.

'Well, here she is, and no harm done,' fawned the demon. 'I only took her away to spoil the priest's endless sacrifices to the gods because a householder's offerings have no merit, as you well know, without his wife beside him.'

The concerned parties went their way cheerfully after that but not the king. He felt ashamed of how he had treated his queen, never making the attempt to understand her while expecting her to run like a well-oiled yantra and sending her away in that brutal fashion.

'Where is she now?' he asked a rishi in the forest, known to be an adept in the supernatural arts. The rishi looked inwards, and out again with a worried face.

'Kapotaka, king of the serpents, kidnapped Queen Vahula when he found her alone in the forest by your order and took her to the netherworld. He would have assaulted her, too, but his own daughter, Nanda, saved the queen and hid her away in a secret cave. She lost her powers of speech for doing so, cursed by her angry father,' revealed the rishi and advised the king on the best route to the netherworld.

Having made his way with great difficulty to the serpent kingdom below, King Uttama stormed Kapotaka's citadel and challenged him to single combat. A mighty struggle ensued but the determined king had the best of it. 'Where is my queen?' he demanded of the cowering serpents, and a richly dressed young serpent maiden stepped forth and gestured to him to follow her. 'This must be Princess Nanda, who saved Vahula,' thought Uttama, following her to the secret cave where his queen was hidden away. He gathered his wife to him with concerned, affectionate words and manfully asked her to forgive him. At this, the queen found herself unable to hold a grudge and spoke to him with renewed love.

The king prepared to return, but Queen Vahula said, 'Stay. Our debt is unfulfilled. My friend Nanda lost her voice because she saved me. We must conduct a Sarasvati Puja for her sake, to beg the goddess to restore her speech.'

'We can do that better at home, let's take Princess Nanda back with us,' urged King Uttama. And all was made well on earth for the brave, good serpent princess, who was able to go home to her now-sorry father in perfect safety, while the king and queen lived happily to the end of their days…

Know, therefore, Kraustuki, said Rishi Markandeya, that a husband has many duties, but chiefly, moral gallantry.

5

Be Nice, You Never Know

The *Panchatantra* was written in Sanskrit by Vishnu Sharman perhaps in the third century BCE. It is a five-part collection of stories-within-stories, drawing on the older oral tradition of the country. Vishnu Sharman is said to have composed it at the request of a king to educate the king's five dull sons. However, some time after the *Panchatantra* first appeared and grew popular in India it took on a life of its own. Around 570 CE, Burzoi, physician to Anaushirvan Khusro, the emperor of Iran, translated the *Panchatantra* into Pahlavi (Middle Persian). This was next translated into another old language, Syriac, by the priest Buda as *Kalilag-Damnag*. The title came from 'Karataka' and 'Damnaka', two jackals in a *Panchatantra* story. Buda's translation became

> *Kalila wa Dimna* in Arabic in 750 CE. The *Panchatantra* went on a long journey after that into Greek, Hebrew, Latin, Dutch, Danish, Icelandic, Spanish, Italian, French and English. This interesting tale from the *Panchatantra* about how a political pickle was created and resolved is retold in tribute to the practical good sense of the old storytellers of India.

Gorambha, the head sweeper at the palace, was very tired. The king of Avantika, like his faithful subjects, had rigorously observed the annual Pitrpaksh or sixteen days of holdback on meat, drink, spicy food and a few other things, to ritually remember his pitris or ancestral spirits with offerings and prayers. But from the day after Pitrpaksh, it was open season. Everybody looked forward to the feasts and celebrations immediately after the solemnities and mutterings of Pitrpaksh were over, for now they could have as much fun as they pleased, get married, buy jewellery, land and new houses, with the astrological licence renewed. The royal palace had been no exception to the tradition of the post-Pitrpaksh party and Gorambha was worn out cleaning up afterwards. How many pots of liquor had the courtiers drunk and how much roast meat had their platters been piled with?

Only one man had behaved with moderation through

the feast and that was the king's favourite minister, Dantila. Gorambha, who observed everybody and everything as he went from room to room with his minions dusting, sweeping and swabbing behind him, approved of Dantila. Was there a more sober, sensible and fair-minded man in all the janapadas, the kingdoms and republics of the north? He doubted it. The kingdom of Avantika ran smoothly and with due process because of Dantila. He was sympathetic to the rightful needs of every citizen but did not tolerate any nonsense. Dantila especially disdained bribery and corruption as utterly beneath him.

'It's really another kind of vanity,' thought Gorambha cynically, 'but the most useful kind to have. Dantila understands that high moral ground is the only place to live if you want to get your way and he's willing to pay the price of self-restraint for it. It keeps him safe from the usual low cunning of politics; nobody can find any mud to throw at him. Not many people understand this but I do from my place. I can see it all happening so clearly.'

And this afternoon was the wedding lunch for Dantila's daughter. He, Gorambha, had been invited, too, as a palace official. Gorambha dismissed his minions and went to wash and change into a new tunic for the party.

He made his way to Dantila's house, curling the ends of his moustache.

There it was, a fine mansion decorated with strings of marigolds and mango leaves and young banana trees tied to the gateposts in welcome. From either side of the gate, an elephant from the king's own stable, lent for the occasion, cleverly sprinkled flower-water on the guests who passed through into the courtyard.

Rows of couches covered in crimson and mustard yellow patterned cloth had been set up in the courtyard. The place milled with nobles, ministers, merchants, foreign guests and important citizens. Going in, Gorambha suddenly felt an immense wave of fatigue wash over him and sat down on a corner of the nearest couch. He felt better almost at once for that and began to look about him at the guests, enjoying their fine clothes, turbans and jewels, spotting people he knew – the heads of the noble clans, their grown-up sons, the palace officials – and giving the foreign guests a thorough once over. How pale the yavana envoy looked and how keenly the Tajikas from over the snows observed the cream of Avantika society.

However, he was so engaged in looking at others that he failed at first to notice the commotion at his own elbow. Dantila's estate manager stood frowning at him while two of his assistants told Gorambha to get up at once. 'You're sitting where the king's relatives are meant to sit. Please get up at once,' they repeated. A few nobles turned to look at the stir. Gorambha stood up in embarrassment. He looked around for Dantila. The king's uncle had just arrived and Dantila had gone up to welcome him. Gorambha caught Dantila's eye and saluted him from where he stood. But Dantila just waved his hand dismissively and turned back to the king's uncle.

The estate manager and his assistants looked meaningfully at Gorambha. Gathering his dignity, Gorambha strode out, head held high. Too angry to go home at once, he walked down to the banks of the Shipra and glared at the river that leaped and sparkled playfully as it flowed by. 'I'll fix that rude Dantila,' he swore and, being gifted with his own cleverness, thought out a foolproof plan that made him chuckle heartily. He went home immensely cheered.

Whereas his team cleaned the rest of the palace, the royal apartments were under Gorambha's personal care. The next morning, he went in early as usual into the king's bedchamber but this time he did not set to work quietly. He groaned, hiccuped and clattered about. When he saw the king's eyes flutter, he muttered loud enough to be heard, 'Ah, fine doings. My royal master sleeps innocently while the minister Dantila romances his queen.'

The king shot up in bed. 'What did you just say?' he barked at Gorambha, who cringed humbly. 'Forgive me, Majesty. I had too much to drink last night and sat up late, gambling. I don't know what idiocies I mumbled.'

The king snorted and lay down again while Gorambha hastily finished and left, his work done in more ways than one. The seed of suspicion he had planted in the king's mind immediately put forth shoots, leaves and branches and shot up into a full-grown tree with deep roots. In barely ten minutes, the king, who was not very bright himself though bright enough to have appointed a capable person like Dantila to run the kingdom, had made it grow with his own insecurities. Gorambha had nicely calculated his royal master's likely reaction.

'The fellow goes into every room in the palace and sees everything. The only other person in the kingdom to have such unlimited access is Dantila. He's a fine-looking man, too, and very well spoken. Look how he has me wrapped around his thumb. What if he's been flirting with the queen on the sly? Would she betray me? No, she would not, her character is too noble and, besides, she loves me. But that rogue Dantila may have tried his luck. Well, he's not going to get another chance,' fumed the king.

He tore out in a royal rage and issued orders that Dantila was to be barred from ever entering the palace again and called for the commander-in-chief of the army. 'Senapati,' he boomed at the startled general, 'you will take on the former minister Dantila's duties today in addition to your own.'

'But, Majesty, I am not a civil administrator,' said the panicked general, a worthy old warhorse on the field but with almost no understanding of namby-pamby soft-living civilians.

'There's nothing to it. Any fool can do it. Any fool just did. A canny soldier like you will do a better job of running the state with efficient precision,' said the king airily and that took care of that.

Nothing was heard of Dantila's reaction to this shattering diktat. He was close-mouthed about his dismissal and calmly set about reordering his town house. He made long visits to his orchards and farms, where he put in place a new, improved system of irrigation that conserved water. He took his family on a pilgrimage to Kashi and other holy places, celebrated every festival as though he had no care in the world and generally added to the already established perception that here was a true karma yogi of the good old sort who did his duty unattached to awards and rewards – the very person described in the Bhagavad Gita who responded to life's ups and downs with utter equanimity.

Meanwhile, the kingdom systematically fell apart. The senapati, not knowing any other way to be, treated the civil administration, the merchants' guilds and the artisans' guilds, the rice farmers' association and the market gardeners' association and even the powerful courtesans' guild, which knew every secret in the city, as though they were raw recruits to the army and he their drill master. He even rubbed the priests of the Mahakaleswar temple the wrong way. This was quite an incredible thing to have accomplished, for these pale, silent men with hooded eyes and shaven heads with only a tuft on it were a mysterious, almost sinister brotherhood. Their pools of patience were infinite, having dealt for centuries with every kind of ruler and political situation and with impossibly heavy pilgrim traffic to the grand old shrine from all over the land. They were deeply networked across the kingdoms and even overseas, and had seen everything and met everybody.

Nobody liked to disturb them for, though they never carried arms, they were known to play a very long game and were implacable in their anger if once roused. Gorambha knew their ways well and could have shared a few useful points with the general had he thought to ask. But no, the general had actually summoned the head priest to his office and curtly demanded that he submit a record of the temple procedure for review, with a view to improving its efficiency. The head priest had courteously inclined his head and gone away without a word. Soon after that, a number of key palace officials had sent in applications to say that they were sick and required long leave with immediate effect. The applications had certificates attached from the best-known physicians of the city. It was a strike without openly being one and brought all kinds of important official work to an abrupt halt. A mysterious fire broke out in the accounts department and a number of important palm leaf records vanished in the confusion, which meant that the revenue collectors were unable to compute that year's budget. Because of this, all sanctions of state funds were held up for repair work on dams, bunds and canals, which led to a loss of crops and protests by the farmers and traders.

The state granary's records went missing next and the officials threw up their hands and complained to the king that they could not carry out any distribution work except on an ad hoc basis.

Naturally, the public began to offer bribes to get their work done, which began to be accepted as they had not when Dantila ran the kingdom. The police gave vent to its natural brutality while the judges, now on the take from the merchants' guilds, had no time for ordinary complainants. Thieves and vagabonds from other kingdoms began to migrate to Avantika as news spread of its supportive atmosphere for their professions. The general sent battalions marching from one end of the kingdom to the other in a show of strength to frighten the public into good behaviour but the citizens proved equal to it. Acting upon orders from unknown sources received by the headman of every sector, citizens and villagers came out to line the streets and highways, and cheered as the marching soldiers went by. They even made their wives and daughters throw flower petals on the path. The moment the soldiers had gone past, however, the public fell back, laughing, into its disorderly ways.

Avantika, once a gem among janapadas, was now the laughing stock of the world. At least three important trade delegations wound up their offices there, complaining of intolerable levels of local malpractice. The balance of trade dipped alarmingly.

'Just one bad monsoon will finish off Avantika, that's all it will take, one bad monsoon. Unless the bureaucratic freeze on funds is sorted the troops will soon rebel or desert. They're basically farmers when they're not fighting, and the countryside is also in such a mess that they will have to leave the army, where their pay is in arrears, to at least save their fields. And with our army reduced like that we will be invaded easily,' predicted the street soothsayers.

Gorambha, too, was disturbed by the general's doings. 'He has unleashed everybody's inner demons, which did not dare come out when Dantila was in charge,' he thought unhappily. 'But Dantila deserved the trick I played on him, so I'm not sorry. *My* job is safe forever, anyhow.'

Matters came to a head on the king's birthday when the king went out in procession on the royal elephant with the general on the elephant behind him, which had once been Dantila's place, and the people of Avantika, or perhaps it was the migrants, actually booed in scorn. The royal party was greatly embarrassed while its escort of guards grinned openly. Dantila heard of it in great detail from his neighbour, the head of one of the oldest families in Avantika, and shook his head. Something would have to be done even if he risked losing face.

Dantila set off resolutely next morning for the palace. As expected, he was stopped at the gate by the guards who said, 'Sorry, sir, but you're not allowed to go in. The king's orders!'

'Please let me speak to him, it's very important,' pleaded Dantila, driven by loyalty to country if not to king. It was high time he discovered why the king was upset, and offered his services to sort out the mess.

Gorambha, who had wandered by just then, could not

resist a gloat. 'Hah, so the great Dantila is being shown the door, is he, as he once showed me the door at his daughter's wedding?' he said loudly.

Dantila immediately understood what had gone wrong and why, and turned to leave without another word.

He sent for Gorambha that very evening. The messenger Dantila sent to Gorambha delivered the invitation with exquisite politeness, exactly as coached.

When Gorambha arrived, with the hint of a swagger, Dantila received him cordially and made him sit on a well-covered seat. A maid served Gorambha a silver glass of mango juice and sweets and savouries on silver plates after which Dantila got down directly to the business at hand.

'Please accept my apologies,' he said warmly to Gorambha. 'I was rude that day and I repent of it sincerely.'

'Yes, I was very hurt,' said Gorambha, his eyes kindling with remembered wrath. 'I was so tired cleaning up after that dinner at the palace that I sat in those reserved seats by mistake. I would have gone and sat elsewhere without a problem had I been treated politely. I remember thinking how you were the only person the previous night at the king's party with some self-control. The other ministers and even the nobles ate and drank too much and made such a mess throwing bones around. I admired you greatly and looked forward to the feast at your house. So I did not expect you, of all people, to…'

'You were my guest as much as anybody else. I think I was very tired myself with so much going on, and unaccountably forgot my manners. I can understand that you were angry enough to somehow have me barred from the palace,' said Dantila quietly.

'I should not have done it. Look at the state of our country now,' said Gorambha sadly.

'I know. That's why I felt it was my duty to try to speak to the king. Nothing else would have made me go back to the palace,' said Dantila.

'I made you feel as bad as I did.'

'Yes, you certainly did that,' said Dantila ruefully. He picked up a fine new set of clothes in silk that had been kept beside him and ceremonially presented them to Gorambha. 'Please accept this, with my sincere apologies.'

'Thank you. I will get you back into the palace tomorrow, see if I don't,' said Gorambha, a touch boastfully.

He went away with his good opinion of Dantila restored. 'The minister is a just man, after all,' he thought as he went home. 'Now let me see how I can make the king dance to my tune again.'

The next morning, when Gorambha entered the king's

bedchamber he broke at once into groans and clankings. 'What a funny king I have. He eats cucumbers sitting on the chamber pot,' he muttered when he saw the king begin to wake.

'What?' said the king, almost tumbling out of bed. 'What did you say, you insolent fool? What a stupid lie. As if anyone would…as if I would. When did you see me do that, liar?'

'Majesty!' said Gorambha in assumed terror, falling to his knees. 'Forgive me! I was very drunk last night, gambling late. I don't know what I may have said, my head hurts so.'

'You are a fool who talks utter nonsense. Mend your ways if you want to keep your job,' said the king sharply and Gorambha finished his work in an apologetic hurry. 'I give him till after breakfast,' he chortled silently as he went away.

The king was noticeably absent-minded through his bath. He could barely focus on his prayers and ate almost nothing of his morning meal. He cast a frowning glance or two at the queen from behind his plate.

'Did Dantila ever…bother you?' he asked at last when the palace maids were out of earshot.

'That good man! What a peculiar thought. Where do you get such ideas from?' said the queen icily.

'No, no, it was nothing. I miss him, you know,' said the king in a hurry.

The queen, who was a regular devotee at and keen patroness of the Mahakaleswar temple, looked at the king speculatively from under her lashes.

'You never like to talk about work so I've been wondering how to ask you…what did he do to make you dismiss him overnight? The kingdom is in turmoil without him and the throne has lost its lustre, a little,' she said.

The king reddened and hung his royal head, a little.

'Well, it was just an experiment to see if we were better off as a military state,' he lied. 'I've been meaning to ask him to come back.'

'I suggest you do so at once. The forenoon is the most auspicious hour today,' said the queen matter-of-factly and went away to worship at the temple and update the head priest.

~

With the royal reconciliation graciously seen through by both parties, and the general given leave to pack his bags for a foreign posting as ambassador to the kingdom of Srivijaya across the eastern seas, it took Dantila about six months of brisk course correction to set Avantika right. He was greatly helped in this by the fact that all lost official documents were mysteriously returned after he came back to power and that every last absentee officer recovered overnight from his long illness and came back on duty. Law and order were restored with a firm hand, repair work was prioritized on a war footing and motivational speeches about best practices in civic life flowed forth from every headman with an eloquence never heard before. Punishments were meted out now and then to show that the state meant business and the trade delegations were warmly welcomed back.

When he was satisfied that his country had been pulled up to a reasonable level of order, Dantila, with the king's permission, threw a party at home for the ministers, department heads and officials who had been critical to regaining control. Gorambha was duly invited as a palace official and this time he was given his share of importance so that he went home entirely pleased. As insurance, though, Dantila secretly planted his own man in Gorambha's team of underlings, who soon insinuated himself into the post of being the crown prince's exclusive cleaner, blocking Gorambha's possible future influence in that quarter. But Dantila never had trouble with the king again. He also served as the crown prince's mentor for many years after he became king. He never forgot to send Gorambha a basket of fruit and sweets every New Year in a pact of continued goodwill, flatteringly addressed 'To a Patriot'.

6

Pork and Spittle

The Tamil canon honours sixty-three saints from a wide cross-section of castes and professions for their intense devotion to Shiva. This twelfth-century parable about the extreme devotion of Kannappan, a hunter, is found in a book of Shaiva saints called *Periya Puranam* or Great Story. It was written by the rich agriculturalist-turned-minister Sekkizhar for his royal patron, the young king Kulottunga Chola II (1133–50). Kulottunga was greatly attached to the Shiva temple at Chidambaram, where he chose to be crowned instead of at the old Chola capital of Pazhaiyarai. He spent a lot of money adding to the Chidambaram temple after he became king. Sekkizhar is said to have narrated this tale to further inspire Kulottunga's commitment to Shiva worship and to include heroic tribal saints within the fold. Kannappan is venerated by all castes even today as an important Shaiva saint and there are statues of him at major Shiva temples.

Sivakocharya was a priest who considered himself an authority on all matters related to his chosen god, Shiva. He was an expert in the *agama* or traditions of Shaiva lore. Long before the great temple to Shiva came up at Kalahasti, where Shiva is worshipped as the element 'air', there was a shrine hidden there in the green folds of the hills – a simple stone shivling in a forest glade. Sivakocharya had discovered it in the course of a long hike through the hills and had made it his business to go there every Shivratri to offer it flowers and water.

It was a bit of a climb up into the hills from his village but the priest did not grudge the effort. In fact, he felt highly gratified to be the one to make the offering to this shrine in the wild and looked forward to the monthly pilgrimage. He always came home flushed with pride and happiness, with the air of having accomplished an especially dear mission. After a wash and the evening meal, the priest loved to discourse to as many village folk as cared to hear him about the serene woodland shrine and its air of untouched purity. 'You almost expect to see

Shiva with Uma Devi at his side strolling through those woods,' he'd say. 'Wouldn't you all like to come with me and see it? I don't want more than four at a time, though; it would disturb the peace of the forest.'

'Yes, in our next life. Do you think we have the time to be loafing about the hills like you?' jeered the villagers good-naturedly and Sivakocharya shook his head at them.

'You don't understand the nature of god-love,' he would say pityingly.

'And what might that be?' someone would invariably ask.

Sivakocharya tried to find the right words but while there were hundreds of devotional verses to choose from, each more poetic than the one before, he wanted to say it right, in the sense of its being something that he felt and could describe in his own words. The best he could come up with was, 'Inside us there is something that has no name and that is where this love lives, that is the part of me that yearns for the beauty of God.' But though he longed to make them understand, he thought it was a very simple way to put it and lacked the courage to use those words.

'And does God love us back?' someone else would say in jest.

'I don't know; but whether God needs my love or not,

I need to love God. If equal affection cannot be, let the more loving one be me,' Sivakocharya would say with finality and the theology was over for the night.

The next month, Sivakocharya simply flew up the hillside borne on his longing to see his god in the forest. Almost trembling in happy anticipation, he stepped around a wild moringa tree and into the glade where the shivling stood under a thriving bel, Shiva's favourite tree.

A cry escaped him and he dropped his basket of flowers and small copper pot of water. A great side of raw pork richly marbled with fat lay oozing blood at the base of the shivling and gobs of dried spittle adorned the shivling's crown. Wild jungle flowers lay slung rakishly in a garland athwart it.

'Desecration!' cried the priest and set to frantically cleaning up the abominations with his own upper cloth. He poured the little water that remained on the shivling, said a prayer in an unsteady voice and made his way home deeply disturbed, resolving to return with cleaning cloths and more water.

Sivakocharya trudged up the hill the very next day, unable to wait until the next Shivratri. To his utter horror he saw that a new joint of meat had replaced the old one, more spittle had fouled the shivling and a clumsy new garland had replaced the old one which had been flung aside to rot.

'Who is this bandit, this hooligan?' he cried despairingly and set to work cleaning away the polluting offerings. 'Lord, if you but had a father and a mother, would you have to suffer these indignities? Did you not bear the lash of the overseer's whip at proud Madurai when you stood in for the poor old lady who was too weak to work on the Vaigai embankment? Every household there was ordered to supply one worker for the repairs or face fines and punishment. But the old lady had no one to send in her place and no money to hire someone and so you went instead, to save her from prison. What do you not do for those who love you? And this is how you get treated in return!'

Weeping in outrage, Sivakocharya went home exhausted, his thoughts in turmoil. 'I usually get there in the afternoon but those offerings were made in the morning,' he said to himself. 'I must get there very early tomorrow and hide and wait to catch the culprit.'

Taking a stout stick with him, Sivakocharya set off next day at the early hour of Brahma Muhurtham itself, which is to say he left home at four in the morning when it was still dark. Stumbling up the hill, tripping over roots and rocks, he made his way with great difficulty to the shivling and hid, panting, behind the moringa tree, where he soon dozed off, fatigued by his rigours.

It must have been about ten in the morning when he was woken up by the sound of someone spitting vigorously on stone. 'Thoo! Thoo!' went the unlovely sound, followed by a loud cough.

'Water for you!' said a triumphant voice. 'And don't you like this nice, plump junglefowl? I couldn't kill a wild boar today, you know, like last time. What about the wild jasmine, eh? See how much I managed to stick in my hair to bring along to you. Now you'll want me to make you a garland of them. Wait, here's some string I've made by plaiting grass. Now, if I had one big red flower to put in the middle of these white ones, how well it would look with the green leaves between. But there were none on the way, though I looked, I can tell you.'

Sivakocharya rose unsteadily, dropping his stick from suddenly nerveless fingers. A big, wild hunter most dangerously armed with an axe, a knife and even a bow and arrows. 'He could kill me easily,' he thought but crushed this worm-like thought. 'You there!' he said, stepping authoritatively out of cover. 'You, with your rude devotions. Blasphemy, utter blasphemy! Stop it at once.'

The hunter looked up amazed. 'What have I done wrong?' he asked in genuine bewilderment.

'Spit, instead of water, meat instead of fruit, flowers polluted by the touch of human hair…don't you know you're doing it all wrong?'

The hunter's face crumpled in dismay. 'I love Sivaperuman, my lord Shiva,' he said with dignity. 'I would never be rude to him or hurt him. I was so happy to find his shrine in the woods. I just did the best I could having seen how people worship him at the villages where I go to trade.'

'Well, take care not to pollute the lord with pork and spittle,' said Sivakocharya stiffly and turned to go but with the oddest feeling that he had intruded, like a wild bear, on something important and private, for he was sensitive to atmosphere although he had acted out of the only notions he had of right and wrong.

The feeling persisted through the evening and that night Sivakocharya was visited in a dream by Shiva himself with his consort Uma Devi by his side. The lord said to him, 'You need to see for yourself how wrong you are about my hunter. His name was Deenan and he haunted my temple at a certain village. One day, when an earthquake shook the temple, everybody else ran out screaming to save themselves. Do you know what Deenan did? He flung himself on the shivling – to save *me*. He's been known as "Dheeran", the brave, since then. Come back tomorrow morning to the forest and I'll show you how much Dheeran loves me.'

Back went the priest next day and hid in a new place from where he could see the shivling without being seen. The hunter came up soon after and saluted the shivling respectfully. This time he bore flowers in his hands and carefully held a leaf-cup of water, which he poured out devoutly. But suddenly, he leapt back with a scream of fright.

'Lord, your eye bleeds!' he cried in grief and, to the watching priest's horror, whipped out his knife from his rude leather belt and set it against his own eyeball. The priest looked at the shivling and almost screamed aloud himself. A thick trickle of bright red blood was indeed oozing from the shivling's right 'eye'.

'Wait just a moment. Take my eye in place of yours,' said the hunter and before the priest could blink he had neatly gouged out his own eyeball with the practised hand of an expert dismemberer of birds and beasts. He placed it tenderly in the carved stone dent that was the socket of the shivling's 'eye'. The hunter's eyeball now stared out ghoulishly from the shivling and the surreal trickle of blood slowly stopped. The priest's stomach churned at the bizarre sight.

Barely had the hunter uttered a happy sigh of

satisfaction at the success of his operation when he screamed again. 'Your other eye! Your poor other eye, it's bleeding, too!' he cried in despair.

There followed a terrible silence in the forest. The priest watched, as though in a nightmare, the hunter step up to the shivling, place his big toe on its second bleeding eye to mark the place and lift his knife to his own remaining eye.

'Don't let him do it, don't let him do it. Sivaperuman, stop him. He loves you! He loves you! I was wrong, I was rude. I'll ask his pardon. Just don't do this,' prayed Sivakocharya as hard as he could.

Unable to wait for God to show his hand, he ran out of cover and fell at the hunter's feet, crying in a frenzy of remorse, 'Please don't hurt yourself. God will be well; he's God, isn't he? But you mustn't hurt your other eye, you absolutely must not, please don't.'

The hunter froze, his action arrested, and the hand with the knife fell.

A laugh rang through the glade, making both devotees jump.

'Blink your eyes, Dheeran,' said a voice gently.

The hunter obeyed – and screamed for the third time, but in joy. 'My other eye is back! Oh my God!'

'That's right,' said the voice pleasantly but with an undertone of iron. 'Now my Dheeran is well again, and you, my other devotee, no less sincere, but perhaps a bit limited, are hopefully wiser about who loves who and how much.'

The hunter and the priest threw themselves full length on the floor of the forest in salute to the shivling.

'We hear you, Lord,' they quavered together.

'Be friends,' said the voice and faded out. The harrowing miracle was thankfully over.

Sivakocharya apologized handsomely to Dheeran and insisted on taking him home.

When they got to his house, Sivakocharya made all the customary guest offerings to Dheeran. He washed his feet and fetched him water to drink, and fruit and buttermilk, and oil to rub on his feet and a fresh set of clothes. Meanwhile, he set about organizing a big impromptu feast and invited every single person in the village.

He introduced Dheeran with honour, related the day's amazing events, gave everyone their exclamatory due and bade them feast.

After they had eaten their fill, the villagers gathered eagerly for the evening chat around Sivakocharya and Dheeran. Everyone wanted to hear the two miracle-men speak, but all they got out of the priest was, 'The Lord himself commanded us to be friends. What more do you want from me? Ask him, he has more to tell you than I.'

The villagers questioned Dheeran about his family and his childhood and learned about the earthquake and how his name had been changed from Deenan to Dheeran. As the evening wore on, the villagers grew increasingly familiar with the guest and lapsed from their exalted religious mood into their normal easy ways salted with jokes and sarcasms.

'Our priest will never tell us what exactly he means by god-love,' said the barber by and by. 'He blushes and hangs his head as though he was in love with some woman that his wife knows nothing about. Maybe you can tell us, Dheeran,' he said and laughed heartily. Several others laughed with him. But as always, the priest said nothing. He looked hopefully at Dheeran. Perhaps his new friend, with whom he had shared such incredible experiences and convulsions of feeling, would do better than he.

The villagers looked expectantly at Dheeran.

'I'm not sure what I can tell you except that I talk to God all the time,' began Dheeran slowly. 'I don't know why I love Sivaperuman or how it began. I just know that there is a part inside me that has no name and that is the part that loves him and sees his beauty everywhere and in everyone, and wants to keep him close and tell him everything.'

A deep silence fell on the gathering, the best tribute to Dheeran's heartfelt words.

The priest gazed at Dheeran wonderstruck. How had his own most sacred thoughts about God, locked in the deepest chamber of his heart, been spoken aloud by the hunter as if by divine insight? 'How blind I have been,' thought Sivakocharya, 'and how fitting the Lord's punishment. Well is he called the Great Player – always delighting in some drama with us deluded ones. I must find the words now to pay Dheeran the spiritual debt I owe him.'

'You gave your very eyes to God,' he said with sudden inspiration to the hunter, 'and we hereby name you "Kannappan", the hero who gave his eyes to God.' The villagers cheered as one man and that became Dheeran's third name for evermore, the name that made him immortal.

7

Hell's Bells

This fable from the Sanskrit compendium *Hitopadesa* is a paean to common sense and mother wit, for '*hit*' means 'welfare' and '*upadesa*' means 'advice' in Sanskrit. It was authored more than a thousand years ago by Narayana Pandit. He said he was indebted for a number of stories to the *Panchatantra*, the older collection of stories composed by Vishnu Sharman to teach worldly sense to five dull princes. Narayana mentioned that he too had written these tales for a similar reason for a king called Dhavalchandra. Nothing more is known about that king or his sons. But Narayana's tales remained to instruct the willing, translated in several Indian languages. This ancient anthology proved very popular with both the Mughals and the British, who commissioned translations from the Sanskrit into Persian and English respectively. After that, the stories from the *Hitopadesa* seem to have found their way into any number of the world's languages and into several English retellings, like this one – may Narayana Pandit chuckle at this version of his version.

It was another lovely October morning by the banks of the Brahmaputra. The mighty river spread out as it flowed by the teak forests in the plains and the little village, like a little village is oddly expected to, snoozed beside it in the afternoon heat. The only sounds to be heard were gentle snores, the rattle of cane hand fans being languidly whisked around on their handles, the occasional moo of a cow and the faint rustle of delicate panels of birch bark paper as the village priest tried to catch up on his manuscript of devotional verses to the goddess between morning and evening service at the temple.

Oh, and the rattle of beads on the foreign abacus as Chatura the curd seller did her weekly accounts. Chatura had given a fat young calf for it to the trader who went every year past their village and into the far uplands along the river's higher reaches, passing from teak forests to pine forests and across the far snows to trade on the other side. He had brought the abacus back with him months later from 'over there' and Chatura had demanded to know what it was – and when he explained, made her bargain.

The men and women of the village had laughed at her but the priest had given her a sharp stare and pursed his lips. Later, when she went to the temple to make her Friday offering to the goddess, he had tried to get the abacus for himself. 'What do you need that foreign toy for, let me buy it for my children to play with,' he had said casually. It was Chatura's turn to give him a sharp look. 'No, thank you, Gosain, I believe I'd rather keep it,' she had said pertly and skipped away. The village shopkeeper's son had looked hard at it too, but his father had cuffed his head and told him to stick to their own cloth knots and knobs for accounting.

Chatura lived with her old mother and kept a few cows in excellent health from whom she obtained enough milk to set in thick, creamy, sweet curds. She set curds in big and little terracotta pots that she topped with dried leaf covers and parcelled neatly with shreds of banana fibre. She had standing orders, special orders and sudden orders and never seemed to run short. Her father had been a good herdsman and Chatura's mother had made butter, buttermilk and curds from the milk. Chatura, their only child and the gift of their later years, had been a silent, brown-eyed baby with an intelligent look to her, and she learned their skills without a fuss. She had been given a long Sanskrit name, of course, found by the priest, but her name at home was 'Chatura', which means 'clever'.

She finished her accounts and put her abacus away, pleased at how the profits were adding up nicely. 'I can rest now,' she thought and stretched herself out on a grass mat near her snoozing mother. Chatura had barely closed her eyes when the terrible sound broke out. 'Dang! Dang! Dang!' it went unceasingly as though a wild, disorderly force was ringing a giant bell.

Chatura ran out at once and so did as many villagers as could get up and run out fast. They stood in a huddle looking towards where the sound came from.

'The forest!' said the headman at last, feeling that some direction was due from him.

'It's a demon in the forest,' said the priest, looking very afraid. 'That's why we found that mysterious skeleton last month on Sriparvata Hill inside the forest. The demon must have eaten him and has now come closer to human habitation. It will eat us next!'

Chatura cast him a sideways glance and he looked away, knowing that she knew that he had also quickly calculated how much he could charge the village for an exorcism at the temple.

The big feudal lord of the village, cousin to the

headman, came up to the gathering with his soldiers. 'Which brave man or men will go to the forest and kill the man-eating demon?' he bellowed above the din. 'I have a reward for that hero or those heroes.'

But not one man in the village was ready to stick his neck out and neither was the feudal lord's company of armed guards while the hideous sound came and went in terrifying snatches.

Nobody cared to hear Chatura's views. She tried to make her way to the headman to talk to him but the moment she said, 'Please, sir...' the men around him grew sarcastic and waved her away.

'This snip of a girl thinks she's cleverer than any of us!' said one of the headman's hangers-on.

'Wait till she's married, she'll have her so-called brains beaten out of her,' said another villager coarsely and Chatura found that the men had closed ranks and looked angrily at her, a mere girl, for daring to interrupt their important councils.

Chatura retreated in silence and boldly set off unobserved into the forest to reconnoitre, for she had the uncanny trait of preferring fact to fancy. As she drew closer to the sound of the bell, she hid herself as well as she could behind the trees until she came to the edge of a clearing. Chatura almost laughed aloud when she saw the 'demon'. It was a band of monkeys ringing a large iron bell with a pattern around the rim and a gigantic clapper. Chatura almost broke cover peering hard at it.

'Why, I know that bell,' she thought excitedly. 'It's the one at the Brahmapur temple that was stolen last month. I know! The thief must have made his way into the forest to hide. But something must have happened to him on Sriparvata Hill. They do say that tigers come to the other side sometimes...perhaps he was eaten by a tiger and that was his skeleton they discovered? The monkeys must have found the bell and brought it away. And now they've begun playing with it!'

Chatura went home grinning. She'd show those rude, bossy men what a girl could do. The next day she went boldly up to the feudal lord's house and asked for audience.

'And what might you want to see his lordship for, your fine ladyship?' joked the guards.

'Tell him I can finish off the demon,' said Chatura coolly.

'Haha!' laughed the guards but Chatura insisted that they would be sorry if they refused and finally one of them led her into the courtyard where the feudal lord rested heavily on a big cot made of jackfruit wood while a burly man massaged his fat legs with medicinal oil.

'I can kill the demon for you, lordship. But it will cost…at least a hundred gold coins for the preparations and the enterprise,' said Chatura, bowing low and saluting the feudal lord.

'A girl like you! Hmm, hmm. Well, why not, after all? None of the men want to, and that menace must be got rid of. But I want your mother to come here and tell me in front of everybody that you've gone of your own free will and with her permission. I'll give you the money then,' said the feudal lord.

This formality duly completed (Chatura had taken her mother into her confidence and the mother thought it was an excellent scheme), the newly appointed demon killer went home with a bag of gold. The next day, Chatura consulted the priest for what she called Step One: conducting a puja to appease the gods and make them look favourably on her venture.

An auspicious hour was found at once and the village shopkeeper's son, casting Chatura a covertly admiring look, staggered up with a sack of best fruit, best groundnuts and tender coconut halves.

Chatura drew a big circle on the ground before the temple, got the priest to sprinkle holy water on it and arranged the fruit, groundnuts and coconut halves inside the circle as an offering to the gods. She prayed aloud to

Ganapati first for a successful mission and then stretched herself flat on the ground in salute to the goddess in the temple. She asked the priest to draw a bright red tilak on her forehead and also mark it with sandal paste. She asked for a fortifying sip of holy water, which the priest poured ceremonially into her palm and she drank reverently, wiping her damp palm lightly on the crown of her head so that not one protective drop would be wasted. She fell at her mother's feet for blessings and her mother, who felt rather frightened after all, cried convincingly over her and blessed her. Chatura then filled a small sack with the choicest of the choice fruit and nuts and, bidding them all a brave farewell, marched boldly into the forest.

Making her way back to the glade, Chatura scattered the fruit and nuts around and stepped back to hide and watch. After a while, just as she hoped, the monkey band swung chattering into the glade with their new toy. Seeing the treats on the ground, they chattered even louder and began to help themselves to it all while Chatura kept an eye on the big monkey who held the bell and seemed to be their leader. Very soon, the big monkey had joined his troop on the forest floor and begun to crack tender coconut flesh out of the shell. He had to drop the bell to do so and Chatura sent up a quick prayer of thanks that he dropped it at the edge of the glade and not in the middle, among the feasting monkey band.

Racing silently around the glade to where the bell lay forgotten, Chatura quickly muffled its clapper with the empty sack. Hefting up the bell and keeping it close to her body, she quietly found her way back to the edge of the forest. She waited for darkness to fall and stole home safely, carrying her prize, and told her mother everything.

Mother and daughter went to sleep exhausted by the anxiety of it all, but also very excited at the success of Chatura's brave mission.

The next day, they dressed in their best clothes and proudly bore the bell to the feudal lord.

The guards led them in respectfully and Chatura told the feudal lord a fine story about finding the demon – she described it as lean and pale, and extremely tall, with straw-coloured hair – and how she had won him over with sweet words, fruit, nuts and a fair amount of gold, taken the bell back from him on behalf of the temple he had filched it from and persuaded him to go away and never come back.

The feudal lord, his henchmen and the whole village cheered Chatura and, since no more bells were ever heard from the forest and never a skeleton found again on

Sriparvata Hill deep inside it, it was plain to the meanest intelligence that Chatura had done her job well.

She was treated with the greatest respect after that and her fame spread to many villages around. The priests of the Brahmapur temple, to which the bell was returned after its adventures, did a special puja of thanksgiving and purification to welcome back the lost and possibly desecrated sacred property of the gods, for no chances could be taken in such matters and it was best to assume the worst. They gave Chatura and her mother a seat of honour at the puja and the best helpings of the consecrated food from it.

Only the village priest cast Chatura an occasional knowing look as if from one conspirator to another, but Chatura always looked blandly back. When she eventually married the village shopkeeper's son, the feudal lord and the headman sent fine presents of gold coins and bolts of silk and muslin and even stood in ritually for the father and maternal uncle that Chatura did not have. The priest conducted her wedding to perfection and was greatly pleased to receive a very handsome fee for his pains. The knowing glances stopped after that and Chatura and her husband lived to a ripe and peaceful old age. They enjoyed their good fortune thoroughly and made sure to give the poor a decent share of it to the end of their days.

8

Children of the Moon

This tale from the *Hitopadesa* by Narayana Pandit, from around the first century CE, is an animal fable. To have animals as characters in a story instead of people was popular with both tellers and listeners in two ways. For one, it made for an interesting change, and for another, it appealed to all ages. There was a third reason, too, a professional secret that storytellers did not openly share with the public. The secret was that animal fables allowed a storyteller to indirectly advise or criticize real-life people and situations without being openly rude. The charm of the story was counted on to deliver its indirect message to both the quick-witted, who got the message at once, and to the more deliberate thinkers, who did not understand until later that the animal story

> actually contained a useful tip for people. For instance, through this fable about rabbits and elephants, Narayana Pandit tells his listeners that the weakest person can save himself from the biggest opponent by sheer wit. The tale could also be taken as a warning not to underestimate a weak opponent.

Arnava was the littlest rabbit in the Shashaka tribe that lived in the meadows around Plavya Lake deep in the big teak forest. It was a large, lovely lake of pure, cool water with gently sloping banks, well hidden from men, and a most excellent place for the rabbit tribe. The meadows around Plavya Lake were thick with sweet, rich grass and pleasant herbs and flowers. Tender wild pumpkins climbed the trunks of the rose apple trees that thickly edged these meadows before they yielded ground to the big dark trees inside the forest. The rose apple trees generously shed their crisp, juicy, bell-shaped fruit for the rabbit folk to feed on. The pumpkins, too, required only a patient wait to fall, and the young rabbits had a marvellous time playing ball with the smaller ones while the mother rabbits liked to tear up bits of pumpkin rind for their babies to teeth on.

The chief of the Shashakas was a wise old warrior, sinewy and strong, who had safely guided the tribe's destiny for twelve long years. He hoped to live another four years at least, the longest span allowed to a rabbit. His name was Trikarna or Three Ears, though of course he had only two. The name came from the 'wise bump' on his head that had first marked him out as a leader in his young buck days – a bony knob on his crown under the soft fur that let him deliver the hardest knocks in head-butts with other bucks. Trikarna hoped to appoint a good leader in his place before he was gathered to the Moon God, the deity of the Shashakas. But none of the second rung or even the third showed real potential and Trikarna was worried about the tribe's future without him around to get them out of danger – like the time of the forest fire eight summers back. Trikarna liked to anticipate every possibility and had been prepared for that, too.

As soon as he became leader, he had gathered the tribe and proposed radical life changes. 'In my view, every rabbit needs three burrows to be really safe. We have had a good long run of safety so far and may have grown careless. So I propose we each make three burrows for ourselves. One beneath a tree to escape wind and rain; one on the highest point of the ground around us to escape water should the lake overflow and flood the meadows; and one beneath the damp soil on the edge of the lake to escape fire.' And that is what had saved the Shashakas when a forest fire had emerged roaring from the trees and burnt a blackened trail right across the meadows almost up to the rim of the lake before it died out.

Arnava greatly admired Trikarna and shyly lurked around him, hoping to pick up crumbs of wisdom. Trikarna was fond of saying to the Shashakas, 'Think, think. Always think. Every living creature must exercise everything it has been given. Because we have such a safe, pleasant life, our minds don't get much to think about. We have it all – food, water, shelter and plenty of open space to run about in all day. So make it a habit to notice things about the air, water and earth and notice everything you can about other creatures, make friends with them where safely possible, for we are part of everything else. Knowledge is power.'

Following his leader's advice, Arnava, though little, set himself to explore the forest every day. Arnava's mother had died soon after he was born, through carelessly eating a poisonous weed, and so he came and went as he pleased. He even tried climbing trees and found he could manage that surprisingly well, at least up to ten feet above the ground, using his strong hind legs to make calculated leaps from branch to branch where possible. Coming down was much harder though and he often slipped and fell with a painful thud on the leafy forest floor. The nesting birds scolded him noisily at first but soon got used to his gentle, inquisitive face peering harmlessly at them. He even made friends with the bees that lived in a small hive hanging halfway up a leafy dark neem amid the teak thickets. The bees ranged through the forest looking for flowering mango trees in season and far beyond the forest to human habitation where the farmers grew delicious pollinators like mustard, toria gourds and arugula leaves that they called taramira. Arnava liked to lie in the snug crook of a branch and listen lazily to their deep, musical hum. He actually drowsed off once and almost fell to the ground far below.

One day as he lay snoozing on his favourite branch, he was woken up by a mighty roar and rumble. The ground shook and the trees swayed. It was a full-sized elephant herd with ten cows and tumbling, squealing calves in the middle with grizzled old bull elephants as the rearguard. They were led by a massive tusker with not two but four long, wickedly curved, sharply pointed tusks. Arnava clung fast desperately, almost tearing his paws on the bark, while the nightmare thundered by. His heart sank as he saw the elephants headed straight to Plavya Lake, trumpeting joyously as they neared the water. He dared not follow them and waited shivering in fright for at least an hour.

When Arnava did make his way home, it was to a tragic scene of blood spattered on the meadow and hundreds of crushed Shashaka corpses scattered everywhere. Not a living rabbit was in sight. Arnava carefully made his way to his burrow on the high ground, where he found Trikarna in council, surrounded by the tribe.

'What happened?' he whispered to Chandrima, a pretty little rabbit cowering at the edge of the gathering whom he liked very much and had played with since they were babies. Chandrima twitched her nose sadly.

'We were all over the meadow as usual when suddenly there was this loud, crashing sound and huge creatures with giant bodies, long noses, big ears and long, pointed teeth growing out of their heads broke out of the trees. There were at least thirty or forty of them of different sizes but all very much larger than us. The moment they saw the lake, they made a loud, squealing sound and rushed across the meadow to the water, crushing us under their great, heavy feet. Many of us had no time to run away, it happened so fast.'

Arnava felt his throat choke with fear and anger. He crept closer to Trikarna through the trembling bodies of the Shashakas.

'Nothing in our lives could have prepared us for this calamity,' he heard the wise old leader say sadly. 'I have done my best for you so far but I cannot think of a solution now. The elephants have gone into the forest on the other side of the lake after drinking their fill. They will certainly come back tomorrow. Perhaps they were searching for another home. But where will we go? We are helpless against their size and strength. They did not even see us when they crushed us.'

'Should we leave Plavya Lake and find a new home?' asked a buck rabbit doubtfully. There was a loud chorus of protest from the other Shashakas.

'But where can we go?'

'Why should *we* go? This is our home, not theirs!'

'Can't we make them go away somehow?'

'I agree,' said Trikarna. 'There is no better place than Plavya Lake for us. And it's our home, not theirs. They have invaded us and spoilt our lives. They should go, not us. But they are so much bigger and stronger that I cannot think of a solution.'

'What can we do, Trikarna? There must be something,' cried the Shashakas.

'Let us eat our fill in case we can't tomorrow and sleep on it. I want all of you to try to think of a way to reclaim our home and make the invaders leave,' said Trikarna steadily.

The Shashakas turned as a body back to the meadow.

They dragged the corpses of their friends and relatives to the far side and speedily dug a mass grave with their strong forepaws. Having washed themselves in the lake after that heartbreaking task, they ate their fill of grass and pulled out more to take back to store in their high burrows. Weeping wearily when it was all done, they clung to each other and went to sleep.

Tragedy struck the Shashakas with full force again the next day. The elephant tribe trooped back earlier than expected to the lake and rushed in, splashing and spraying each other the moment they were in, churning mud and rolling luxuriously in it. Once again, the rabbits in their path had no time to escape and were left dead and dying in pathetic little heaps of trampled fur, blood and bones.

The remaining Shashakas fled for cover and could not emerge till sunset for the elephants made a day of it at Plavya Lake and showed every intention of settling there for good, coming out to forage on the rose apples, knocking all the pumpkins down and stripping all the younger branches bare of their leaves.

Arnava's heart boiled in rage. He knew the jungle law, as every creature did, that might was right. But every creature also had the right to its life and was fully entitled to fight back for survival. Plavya Lake was his ancestral home. He wanted the satisfaction of knowing before he too was killed that, at the very least, he had tried his best to save his home and his people from the marauders.

Arnava stole out that night from his burrow and looked up at the moon, the guardian deity of the Shashakas. It was the fourteenth night of the moon's bright half. Almost full, the moon shone golden on the waters of Plavya Lake and lit the meadows and forest with heavenly light. Arnava could see the great ancestral rabbit of his tribe enshrined clearly on the moon's surface.

'Help me,' he prayed fiercely with all his little heart and lay down on the grass to think.

~

After consulting with Trikarna next morning, Arnava crept into the forest looking for the elephants. He soon found them, systematically stripping every tree around them of its leaves. He crept as close as he dared to the four-tusked leader whom he heard the other elephants respectfully address as Chaturdanta or Four Tusks, and waited for the big tusker to wander a little away from his herd. When Chaturdanta, with a pleased grunt, stopped by a mango tree and began to break off its most tender and leafy twigs, Arnava, his heart beating fast, climbed the mango tree from the other side until he was almost eye to eye with the tusker.

'Ho, Chaturdanta!' he cried boldly in his loudest voice.

The big elephant was thoroughly startled.

'Who are you that knows my name?' he asked, dropping the bundle of leaves he had just gathered.

'I am the messenger of the Moon God. I have come to tell you that you and your tribe are forbidden to return to the lake. It is the home of the rabbit tribe, who are under the Moon God's protection. You crushed them and killed them in their home every time you went to the lake. The Moon God is angry and wants you to leave this lake at once and find yourselves another home.'

Chaturdanta thought this over slowly. 'That is not good, the Moon God's anger. I am sorry we killed the tribe under his protection; we did not even see them. We elephants do not shed the blood of other creatures. We eat grass, leaves and fruit and mind our own business. My tribe has suffered a lot already, for our own pond dried up and we had no water left,' he rumbled. 'We heard of a big lake to the east and marched five days and five nights to get here.'

'I am sorry to hear that and wish you better luck at your next destination. But you must leave this one, those are the Moon God's orders,' said Arnava politely but firmly.

'Take me to the Moon God that I may apologize before we go,' said Chaturdanta sadly, worried for the well-being of his tribe. What if this lake too dried up? Not only had they offended the Moon God but they were guilty of so many deaths, which was completely against the code of the elephant tribe. It was better not to risk another disaster but to move on patiently. There had to be a lake or river elsewhere.

'I can tell you where to go, if you like,' said Arnava, suddenly remembering something the bees had let drop. 'If you keep going east for another five or six days, you will cross this forest and the next one. Beyond that is a river with broad banks on which grow many flowers and much wild grass. You could find a new home there.'

'Thank you. We will stay in this forest today and leave after you take me to the Moon God,' said Chaturdanta.

Arnava thought fast. 'Come tonight by yourself to the lake and I will take you to the Moon God. But do not say too much or disturb him in any way, for he is very upset about the deaths you have caused,' he said.

'Very well,' said Chaturdanta and turned away to warn his tribe to stay in the forest and leave the lake alone.

Arnava scrambled down as fast as he could and raced home to tell Trikarna. The head of the Shashakas warned his tribe to finish their business by the lake well before sunset and stay put in their high burrows after that until he gave the all-clear.

The day passed in great anxiety. As dusk began to fall, the Shashakas made off to their burrows and waited trembling in both fear and hope. Only the little figure of Arnava was to be seen in the meadow, a tiny white blur in the darkening shadows. The full moon rose splendidly golden in the sky. Soon, a massive shape emerged from the trees and Arnava hopped rapidly towards it. 'Come very quietly with me,' he said. 'The Moon God has taken an avatar to come down from the skies to console the families of the dead Shashakas. He is deeply grieved and very angry. It's best that you silently salute him and leave at once.'

Chaturdanta nodded sadly and followed Arnava to the water. The full moon was perfectly reflected in Plavya Lake as though it had indeed taken a second form to come down to earth while its original form remained in heaven to light the world.

Chaturdanta bowed respectfully to the beautiful reflection in the water, saluted Arnava with his trunk in farewell and lumbered silently back into the forest. Arnava went after him quietly to see what he would do next. To his great joy, he saw the elephant tribe lined up in marching formation, waiting for their leader. Chaturdanta spoke softly to them as he went by inspecting the order. He took his place at their head and some indistinct signal passed down the long line of great beasts to the rearguard. The great tusker set off in the direction of the east and the elephant tribe followed him in silence. They disappeared slowly into the teak forest away from Plavya Lake.

A great silence fell on the forest in their wake and all Arnava could hear was his own heart thumping loudly in relief. The danger was gone.

Arnava rushed back to the meadow to tell Trikarna, who was too overcome to do more than pat Arnava on the back. The old leader drew a ragged breath and gave the signal for the waiting Shashakas to emerge.

What a marvellous sight, then, under the full moon, as the whole tribe rushed out to hug their little hero. The Shashakas danced in joy all over the meadow and each rabbit made sure to give Arnava some choice titbit of his or her finding while Trikarna stayed close to Arnava, patting his head every now and then.

'We are a small race and you are the smallest of us, young one,' said Trikarna, as the revels ended and the Shashakas began to leave for their burrows. 'But you used your mind and saved us all and saved our home, worthy child of the moon. Your training starts tomorrow, Arnava. I'm going to teach you everything I know so that you'll make a good leader when the time is right.'

9

The Shower of Gold

Adi Shankara, the philosopher-savant from present-day Kerala, is said to have lived between the fifth and eighth centuries. He is revered as the foremost Hindu reformer. His story was retold in almost every century after him, making a separate genre in Indian literature called *Shankara Vijayam*, the victory of Shankara. The first book on him in English, *The Age of Sankara*, was written a hundred years ago by T.S. Narayana Shastri, in 1916. The legend goes that Shankara became an ascetic at barely eight and died at thirty-two. He braved wolves, brigands, hunger, thirst and fatigue in an epic venture, criss-crossing the jungles and mountains of India from coast to stormy coast, from the farthest south to the high Himalayas. His mission was to unify the splintered religious sects and remake the Hindu religion, clarifying its focus and functioning. Part of this project was to found five ashrams across the country to which he appointed heads from different regions. They were called 'Shankaracharya' or 'Teachers of Shankara's tradition'. The first such ashram was the Sharada Peeth on the banks of the Tungabhadra in present-day Karnataka. In the fourteenth century, its twelfth Shankaracharya was Madhava Vidyaranya, the mastermind behind the creation of the great Vijayanagar Empire. Vidyaranya Swami inspired its first kings, Haka and Buka, in their struggle to found an independent kingdom with parables on Shankara such as this one on courting good fortune for a worthy cause.

Hemavati was a desperately poor woman who lived alone in a hut at the far end of the agraharam or priests' street in her village. Her husband had been a ne'er-do-well who never cared to tend the three home fires – the garhapatya, the ahavanya and the dakshina – to whom a householder had to make offerings in the old days to ensure the peace and prosperity of society. Abandoning his duties, he had left the village tagging along with a band of tantric mendicants and no more was heard of him. Was she a wife or a widow, wondered Hemavati, ironically named 'the golden one'. The village wondered, too, and had many a salty wisecrack to make. Hemavati had no children, she was getting on in years and had no source of income.

Had her husband been around and earned his keep, ceremonially addressing the gods on behalf of those who were born, got married and died, who built new homes, acquired new fields or wanted special rituals conducted, the village would have automatically supported her. Food and clothes would have come her way in return, thought Hemavati, shivering a little as a sudden cold breeze blew in over the agate waters of the river close by, and into her hut. But as a woman alone, she had no standing and no value. She made sure to attend every festival at the local temple where free food was distributed in charity and offered to do the household chores of her neighbours for a bit of rice and old clothes. But after her kindest neighbour died in childbirth, there was nobody in the village who was particularly bothered about her. Her last and only garment was reduced to tatters and there had been absolutely no food in the house for four days now. Hemavati felt ashamed to even step out of her hut in her ragged state. 'I must have done something bad in my last birth to suffer so,' thought Hemavati bleakly, drinking yet more water to fill her stomach.

She went to bed that night on her grass mat spread out on the earth floor feeling very lonely and discouraged. The thatch was falling apart and through the holes in the roof Hemavati could see the Dhruv Tara, the Pole Star, shining steadily in the sky. She went to sleep inexplicably cheered.

The next morning, however, Hemavati was horrified to hear the clear, young voice of a bhikshu or ascetic calling out for alms. What a very young voice for a sanyasi, she thought. She peered out through a hole in the wall. A child of no more than eight or nine in the ochre robe of a mendicant stood outside her rickety wooden door, holding out his alms bowl. 'How very unusual, a child ascetic. How did his parents permit it?' wondered Hemavati, for she knew that a man may not take sanyas, the oath of renouncing normal worldly life, without the formal permission of his parents were they alive.

Staring bemused at the child, Hemavati thought of the dire rules of sanyas.

Anyone could become an ascetic if his appetite for food, sex and worldly doings had vanished and his thoughts and speech had taken an unworldly turn.

After leaving home – his parents, wife, children and worldly goods – a sanyasi had to live outside the village and not in a home of his own, and sleep under a tree or in an uninhabited house, wherever he found himself at sunset.

Unless he was studying with a guru or was a teacher himself, he had to be constantly on the move and was allowed to stay on in a place only during the rains. He was bound to observe strict rules of courteous conduct in his interactions with the rest of society. He was not allowed to ever light a fire, not even for cooking food, but had to subsist on alms.

There were stern rules about begging for food, too. A sanyasi could enter a village or town to beg only once a day. He could only beg from a maximum of seven houses, not selected beforehand. If none of them gave him alms, he just had to do without. He could wait at one house only for as long as it took to milk a cow. He was not allowed to secure his food by interpreting omens, making predictions or reading horoscopes. He was not to eat his fill but only as much as it took to keep body and soul together.

'Such a little boy in such a harsh life that most grown men would be afraid to undertake,' marvelled Hemavati, overcome by the sanyasi's extreme youth and his astonishing tejas or lustrous aura. She wished very much that she had food to give him.

'Alas, young bhikshu,' she called out tremulously to

the waiting child, 'I have nothing to give you. I have had no food myself these several days.'

'Have you nothing at all for me?' said the clear child-voice gently.

'Wait, let me take one last look,' Hemavati found herself saying. She turned over her empty pots, bins and baskets. There lay a single shrivelled amla at the bottom of the last basket. Hemavati pounced on the gooseberry and took it to the door. Opening it only a little way, to hide her ragged state, she put out her right hand with the amla. 'I am so sorry, child, I have nothing at all but this. Please take it, if you don't mind such paltry alms. It would make me very happy,' she said, deeply ashamed, and dropped it into the boy's alms bowl.

Instead of going away, the boy stood looking at the amla with a troubled face. Hemavati heard him draw a deep breath and saw him step back and raise his arms aloft to the sky in salute. He shut his eyes for a few moments as though praying and burst into a hymn of praise to Lakshmi, goddess of good fortune. Twenty-one beautiful verses poured out of him, describing the goddess in whom he said he saw all the goddesses as one.

'Let her garland of glances that protects Lord Vishnu, and gives him great strength, fall on me as well,' Hemavati heard him sing, enchanted. 'Gracious goddess, giver of joy, giver of wealth and giver of the right to rule kingdoms, be merciful as the cool breeze. Shower a rain of wealth on this parched land.'

A gentle breeze blew when the boy finished and a great concentration of light appeared before him, a column of light so bright and intense that it stood out even in the light of day.

'You have pleased me greatly with your sweet, spontaneous song,' Hemavati heard a thrillingly melodious feminine voice say. 'Ask something of me, child.'

'Gracious Mother! Please make this poor lady prosperous, I beseech you,' said the boy ascetic, saluting the column of light.

'I may not do that, son, for she never gave anybody a thing in charity in her last life,' answered the celestial voice.

'Why, Mother, look how she gave away the gooseberry, the very last thing she had in her house. She was starving for days and could have kept it for herself – the first bit of solid food that she accidentally found while looking to feed me. But she gave it away in alms, did she not? Mother, you know very well that you alone have the power to erase and change the destiny written by Lord Brahma on each person's head,' cajoled the child.

Hemavati heard an amused laugh.

'So be it,' said the goddess, and the column of light faded.

The next moment, a hail of hard gooseberries fell through the holes in the roof of Hemavati's hut, each made of solid gold. She would be rich beyond avarice now. Hemavati rushed out to thank the boy ascetic and call him in to see the mound of golden gooseberries.

'Child, I am beyond beholden to you. Please come by again that I may give you proper alms, how else may I thank you? I shall make sure to feed many others, too, in thanksgiving,' she stammered.

The boy ascetic smiled sunnily at her. 'It was very kind of the goddess, was it not?' he said, beaming. 'It's all her doing.'

'What name do you go by, blessed one?'

'Shankara.'

'Forgive me for asking, little bhikshu…but how could your parents bear to let go of you for even a day? How could they actually let you take sanyas and wander so far, alone?'

'My father died when I was very little. And my mother let me go only very recently, only when she thought I was about to die. I had gone for a swim in the river by which I lived and was suddenly seized and almost dragged under by a crocodile, and I cried aloud for her permission to take sanyas with what I thought was my last breath. She agreed out of pity and terror to fulfil what she thought was my dying wish. But when I was miraculously freed, she had to keep her word though she was not happy about it,' said the boy simply and directly.

'God bless you and keep you!' said Hemavati, shuddering at the thought of the child's well-knit limbs being ripped apart. What courage, to call out so, literally from the jaws of death. What a bold, tender-hearted little bhikshu, to address the goddess on another's behalf and in such verse as to make her appear, and then to bandy words with her like that and get his way.

'He is marked for some great work. It was the ochre that chose him, really, and not he who chose the ochre,' thought Hemavati with a sudden flash of insight. However, she was too shaken to say so, overcome as much by the miracle of the golden shower as by the extraordinary contrast between the young bhikshu's magical power and his boyish simplicity. Gathering her wits, she managed to say, 'What a beautiful hymn to the goddess that was. Won't you teach it to everyone who cares, blessed one, that all may benefit...the Litany of the Shower of Gold?'

'I will,' said the boy and went away smiling to fulfil

his destiny while Hemavati watched him go through a mist of grateful tears, secure in the knowledge that her dignity and well-being were splendidly assured.

Note: The Kanakadhara Sthavam or Litany of the Shower of Gold is a hugely popular prayer even today across a wide section of Indian society.

10

A Hundred Pots of Pongal

Adi Shankara, like Buddha, wanted to spare everybody pain by teaching them to look at existence in a detached way. His philosophy of Advaita was that the soul of every living person is actually part of an impersonal mega-soul or Supersoul like the one discussed back in the Upanishads, so why mourn earthly loss and mishap? However, the human need to worship a 'face' proved overpowering and Sri Ramanuja, the influential Vaishnava saint of the eleventh–twelfth century, modified Shankara's Advaita or Non-Dualism into Visisht-Advaita or Qualified Dualism. He proposed the belief that while a devoted human soul could become part of the Supersoul, it was separate and inferior to the Supersoul, who was none but the god Vishnu.

Ramanuja was deeply moved by the legend of the ninth-century girl saint Andal who saw Krishna (Vishnu) as her husband and was believed to have 'merged' into the massive idol of Vishnu at Sri Rangam, the southern centre of Vaishnavism. Sri Rangam was where Chaitanya Mahaprabhu, the fifteenth-century founder of Vaishnavism in Bengal and North India, made the longest stay, during the four months of monsoon called chaturmaas, on his travels to holy places for six years after taking sanyas. He went to the Sri Rangam temple every day on his visit after bathing in the river Kaveri. It seems entirely likely that his host Venkatesh Bhatt told him this popular southern Vaishnava parable which teaches that devotees are 'soul family'.

The great temple of Sri Rangam rose monumentally in the early dawn on its island at the confluence of the Kaveri and the Kollidam. Emerald-green parrots, the messengers of love poetry, swept out in flocks from where they had sheltered for the night between the carvings on its towering gateways. Sleepy temple attendants lit torches in the corners of the courtyard and, within the sanctum, the priests, freshly bathed in the Kaveri, lit the oil lamps within the shrine and arranged the baskets of flowers, the camphor, the incense, the silver pitchers of sandalwood water and rose water for the morning prayer, as the first worshippers trickled in to start their day with a glimpse of Vishnu's great black granite idol. The idol was two-armed and instead of looking west, as all idols did to enable devotees to prostrate east in the direction of the light, it looked south towards Lanka. This was the deity's promise to the mythical king Vibhishan, which had occurred in a dream to the temple builders.

A chorus of bright, young voices was heard approaching from the town, the girls singing as they walked. They had begun at the other end of the neighbourhood and as they went singing from door to door they were joined by more girls waiting for them to come by. The girls were freshly bathed and dressed to go with flowers in their hair and festive marks on their foreheads. As they walked, they sang the eighth-century songs composed by the girl saint Andal.

Those townsfolk who were out and about already smilingly made way for the girls and stopped to hear them sing as they went by in the blue-grey light of the early morning. Soon, great streaks of pink and gold would light the sky and the day would go on as it always did – but these early mornings of the lunar month of Margazhi (mid-December to mid-January) were special to the daughters of the town.

A group of Vaishnava ascetics gathered in the forecourt of the temple waited for the girls to come over the walkway and into the temple. They listened in deep spiritual pleasure as the girls sang Andal's vivid poems of her burning love for Vishnu and her spiritual longing to merge her soul in him. Tears began to flow down the lean, brown cheeks of their leader, Ramanuja, whose name meant 'Ram's younger brother', another name for Lakshman. He had made his own bold journey of love for Vishnu. Born to a Tamil brahmin family in the temple town of Sriperumbudur, he had staked his all on his early conviction that God was infinitely and impartially loving and made no difference between castes. Ramanuja's guru had been furious at what he did when he was taught the powerful secret of the eight-syllable mahamantra 'Om Namo Narayanaya'. The spell appeared to merely state 'I praise Lord Vishnu'. But it contained deep vibrations and had a healing, empowering effect. To be taught the great mantra was a boon and a blessing. Only a deeply learned and spiritually evolved guru could impart this mystic spell, and only to a pupil who was worthy. But what had Ramanuja done with this treasure?

Overcome with ecstasy he had dashed up the gateway

of a nearby temple, climbed perilously to the very top and proclaimed the mahamantra loudly for all to hear. 'It belongs to everyone. *God* belongs to everyone. Don't you see, it must be shared so that every single person can benefit by it,' he had argued afterwards and eventually gone his own way, attracting a growing band of disciples as he travelled the land speaking of Vishnu-love and inspiring men of all castes to participate in renovating old Vishnu temples and building new ones.

'It was the story of Andal that made me see the light,' said Ramanuja as the girls went by, followed by townsfolk carrying great flower garlands in offering to Vishnu. 'How can I ever repay her? She lived over three hundred years before I was born. But see how her spirit lives on through her songs, which these girls sing in such pure, sweet voices. Why would they bother if Andal's utter love for Vishnu had not melted their hearts as it did mine?'

Hoping to achieve this heart's desire some day, Ramanuja and his disciples went on to a place called Yadavadri where they stayed in retreat for some time before he decided to return to Sri Rangam, which pulled him to it as a mother would draw her child close. On the way he stopped to pay his respects at Azhagar Kovil, the temple to Vishnu at Madurai. This was the very place where in another age young Andal had composed a prayer which said, 'O Lord Hari, if you will accept me, I will offer you a hundred pots of sweet rice pudding and a hundred pots of pure white butter.'

Shortly after making her promise there, Andal had gone back to her village, Sri Villiputtur. She had been found out soon after, by her saintly father, in an act of vanity. She had taken to wearing the garland of flowers she wove every day for Vishnu before giving it to her father to offer in worship. One day, her father had spotted a long, black hair caught in the flowers and had made Andal own up. But her father had had a strange dream in which Vishnu had appeared to him and said that it was perfectly all right. It was only Andal's pure and intense love that had made her wear 'his' garland. Events had moved swiftly after that for the young devotee and one day she had gone to the Sri Rangam temple, touched the feet of Vishnu's idol there, swung herself up to sit on them…and disappeared.

Everybody believed this.

The old priest at Azhagar Kovil lovingly recalled the girl saint's promise to Ramanuja and it struck him dazzlingly that this was the perfect way to repay his spiritual debt to Andal. He would keep her promise for her.

Such was Ramanuja's stature that he had barely spoken the thought aloud when the old priest, as impulsively as he himself had once climbed the gateway to proclaim the mahamantra, sprang up and began to ring the temple bells vigorously. The people of Madurai rushed over at once to ask what the matter was.

'The Yatiraj, king of ascetics, wishes to offer a hundred pots of sweet pongal pudding and a hundred pots of butter to keep Andal's promise which was made here long ago, here at your own temple. What do you say?' asked the old priest of his flock.

A roar of approval was his answer. An auspicious hour was fixed for the next evening and the poor were told of the feast in store. Contributions poured in from almost every household and a great public feast was organized to follow the offering.

The next day, looking at the rows of earthen pots of sweet rice pudding and the pots of freshly churned butter, Ramanuja felt a great sense of satisfaction. Although it had happened centuries later, Andal's wistful promise had been well and truly kept. How blessed it felt to see rich and poor seated together in orderly lines to accept the food being served on rows of banana leaves.

Soon after, Ramanuja and his disciples went on to Sri Villiputtur, the birthplace of Andal. They offered prayers at the Vishnu temple there, where Andal had once addressed her burning love poems to her god and tried on the garlands meant for him as though she were his bride.

The atmosphere in this temple was sweet and peaceful and the lane outside was lined with stalls selling palkova, squares of milk fudge that the sellers laughingly entreated Ramanuja to taste. He was startled that they, too, called him 'Elder Brother'. Every single person encountered in Sri Villiputtur had done so from the moment he had entered the town.

Ramanuja went on next to the temple built to consecrate Andal herself and that was where the mystery was explained to him. A band of bright young girls escorted by their mothers accosted him, beaming, as he entered the temple. 'So you have come, Elder Brother, to receive the thanks of your little sister!' they exclaimed and, saluting him affectionately, went their way. The news had raced ahead of him from Madurai to Sri Villiputtur. Ramanuja was left in communion with the stone idol of Andal dressed as a bride, her long hair rolled up to one side, a parrot perched on her uplifted left hand and a magnificent bridal garland of real flowers around her neck.

'Welcome, Elder Brother,' he heard a merry young voice say in his heart. 'You were born years after me but I went away when I was just a little girl. You, as a man grown, have fulfilled my promise out of loving sympathy. You may have been named after Sri Rama's younger brother. But you are Andal's elder brother, are you not? The one she never had – until now.'

Ramanuja's eyes overflowed and he sat for a long, silent while at the foot of Andal's idol, thinking tender thoughts of God and his 'little sister'. A sanyasi had to renounce all earthly relationships when he took the vow of renunciation. But in place of those he actually seemed to find purer bonds with another 'family', those liberated by their shared love of God.

Ramanuja got up, bade Andal farewell and gathered his followers waiting outside. With the easy stride of a man at perfect peace with himself and the world, he set off on the long walk home to Sri Rangam.

11

Death and the Demon King

Meera Bai, the sixteenth-century poet-princess, is believed to have composed at least 1300 poems to Krishna. According to tradition, her in-laws, the royal family of Chittor, fiercely resented her extreme devotion to her chosen deity. They sent her a snake hidden in flowers and a cup of poisoned milk but Meera mysteriously escaped their attempts to kill her. Meera is said to have then had a letter smuggled out of Chittor to Tulsidas of Varanasi, author of the *Ramcharitmanas*, the 'people's Ramayana' which was written in an everyday dialect of Hindi. Since Tulsidas was a fellow devotee of Vishnu, of whom Ram and Krishna were avatars, Meera asked Tulsidas for advice. 'I can't break my bond with Krishna even if I have to endure being constantly

> tortured by my family,' she wrote. In his sensational reply, Tulsidas cited the popular parable of Prahlad, a mythical devotee of Vishnu. Although Meera was a real-life devotee, moreover a delicately nurtured royal widow only in her thirties, Tulsidas advised her to walk out disowning her family like Prahlad had disowned his father.

Hiranyakashyap the demon king was worried. He was an asura, a mighty titan who properly belonged to Patal, the netherworld, the assigned realm of his race. He had schemed and politicked and finally managed to overcome not only the netherworld but also the celestial realm and earth to become the unchallengeable master of all three. And he had nicely bullied that dotard, Brahma, he thought, into giving him the ultimate boon of invincibility.

'Father, Father,' lisped those ridiculous devas, the celestials, when they spoke to Brahma. But not he, Hiranyakashyap. He had undergone such ferocious austerities that the three worlds had wobbled madly when the karmic balance of the universe began to tilt towards him. The devas had gone fluttering, of course, to Brahma to do something about it. But Brahma was in no position to listen to them. No, he had had to come down to where he, Hiranyakashyap, sat in dire penance and had to offer him a boon to stop.

'I don't need you for fighting my battles and crushing my enemies for I crush them as I crush ants under my heel,' Hiranyakashyap had said with a fine sneer, without so much as a salute to the old creator. 'No, what I want from you is utter invincibility. Grant me this – that I cannot be killed by a celestial, a titan or a human, by any weapon ever made, by night or day, not indoors or outdoors, on land, at sea or in the air.'

The creator had looked a little quizzical. 'Are you absolutely sure that you want that?' he had asked in his mild voice.

'Of course, you old fool,' thought Hiranyakashyap. But aloud he had said, 'Yes, I do.'

'So be it. But you may wonder one day if you have chosen well,' the creator had said annoyingly and vanished.

But why was Hiranyakashyap worried? He was the despot of the universe. He was...god. The lord of life. He had issued orders to everyone to worship him with song, dance, prayer and sacrifice. And everyone had obeyed the 'demon king' as the titan was now known. Except, he thought bitterly, the snake in his sleeve, his own son, Prahlad, whose name meant 'an excess of joy' for that is what the entire asura nation had felt at his birth.

How could Prahlad refuse to obey his own father and insist that he would pray only to his chosen deity, Vishnu? A meek child in other ways but not in this. 'Never in this, Father,' he had said calmly, bowing the while. 'My heart belongs to Vishnu. I have to pray to him or else it makes me cross.'

A world of unspoken asura temper there. Hiranyakashyap was strangely pleased about that. 'He hasn't turned into one of those mawkish earthlings, anyhow,' he thought with a frisson of fatherly pride. 'I may win him over yet.' But how?

'Perhaps a tour of the kingdoms, a family outing,' considered Hiranyakashyap. 'A pity the boy's mother is dead and he is polite but distant with my other wives. I'll ask my sister Holika to come along. They like each other.'

There followed many pleasant picnics at the most scenic places in the three worlds. The asura court glittered with royal levees and galas and music concerts, and bewitching performances by the apsaras, the celestial dancers of the deva court who now belonged to the asuras. There were hunts and jousts and competitions in everything likely to interest a sturdy young crown prince – archery, fencing, wrestling and chariot races. And through it all, the twelve-year-old Prahlad, with every appearance of enjoying himself keenly, would retreat every single day at an appointed hour to his tent or his room to pray to Vishnu.

It was all the fault of that busybody Narada, brooded Hiranyakashyap. Narada, the ultimate party-goer with the most frequent flyer miles in the three worlds, a walking library and veena maestro, networked like nobody else and was high on every A-list of invitees. The celestial seer had dropped by suddenly on Patal as he often did when Hiranyakashyap's chief queen was expecting Prahlad. He had stayed on to amuse her and crammed her head with Vishnu lore, of which the baby within had heard every word. And then, when little Prahlad was barely five, Narada had come by again and offered to be his tutor. Flattered by the devrishi's interest, Hiranyakashyap had readily agreed and set up the royal asura nursery as a charming schoolroom. How could he not have noted that the devrishi was besotted with Vishnu and exclaimed 'Narayan! Narayan!' with every other breath, taking that name of Vishnu's many names?

But every last flicker of paternal feeling died out in the demon king during the next big festival in which he was to receive the worship of all his subjects. The demon king's ministers had striven to please by organizing a great public rally with legions from all three worlds marching loyally by. At the critical moment of prostrating en masse to Hiranyakashyap, the new god of gods and king of kings, Prahlad sat it out. He remained on his golden throne, refusing to prostrate at his father's feet. It was too public a rejection to ignore and Hiranyakashyap, like any dictator, was extremely sensitive to public opinion. Snubbed by his son, the crown prince? There would have to be consequences. Hiranyakashyap set about organizing them.

Prahlad was given the customary drink of poisoned milk one night but woke up as well as ever with not even a mild headache in the morning, let alone having horrible dying throes minutes after he had drunk it down. He was pulled out of bed the very next morning and taken away to the royal elephant pit, where he was buried in mud to his neck. A musth tusker, further maddened by many sharp jabs with the goad, was made to stand over the prince and prodded to lift its feet and trample his head. But somehow, the tusker declined and veered away. None of the other royal elephants would cooperate in this task either, and Prahlad was dug out, washed and sent back to his room under armed escort.

Through it all, the prince remained maddeningly calm, murmuring 'Hari, Hari' to Vishnu. Hiranyakashyap was at his wits' end. 'The snakepit,' he thought. 'There's that cliff up in the thorn forest, below which is the cobras' nest.

Let him be thrown down to them. The effect of snakebite is slow and horrible.'

Prahlad was marched there the next day, though found to be strangely drowsy. The soldiers who took him away did not know that his aunt could not bear to think of Prahlad's dying agonies and had drugged his food so that he would fall asleep and not feel the pain.

'Poor fellow, that's a bad death even for an asura warrior,' said the soldiers as they pushed the prince off the cliff.

But next morning, when they carefully lowered themselves to retrieve his corpse, they scattered, screaming, for they saw Prahlad fast asleep on a still mound of snakes that were bunched quietly under him and around him like a mattress. The soldiers clambered back up the cliff and made a big din to awaken the prince; and when he opened his eyes and looked languidly up at them, they lowered a rope for him to climb and took him home without a word.

Hiranyakashyap rushed to his son's apartments to verify this miracle only to find him being petted and fussed over by his aunt Holika. He dragged Holika out in fury and slammed the door on Prahlad.

'How could you want to kill your own son?' asked Holika fiercely when out of earshot.

'You're my sister! You're my subject! You're not allowed to question anything I do!' stormed Hiranyakashyap and then looked appraisingly at Holika. 'He trusts you. And he does not know what I do, that when you were a girl, you were given a magic cloth that would keep you safe from fire. Well, get it out. Tomorrow you're going to get Prahlad to sit on your lap and we'll set fire to you both.'

Holika looked quietly at Hiranyakashyap. 'This is not my brother. It's a power-mad monster,' she thought. 'I can't fight this creature. But I can escape it.'

The next day, Holika led Prahlad to the inner courtyard, carrying a light, soft length of cloth over her arm. 'Let's sit on this nice bench near the lotus pond,' she said. 'Let me put this around you, dear, and hold you a bit. You're a good boy, Prahlad. Your mother was my best friend… and you have her eyes. Well, I can tell her I did my best to look after you.'

Prahlad looked into Holika's eyes. 'Aunt, is Father about to do something unpleasant again?' he asked bluntly.

'Yes, he is. You must keep that cloth around you and not mind anything that may happen. It's all for the best. See how close we are to this pretty lotus pond? How full of cool water it is,' said Holika. Tucking the cloth tightly around Prahlad, she held him close for a moment and then loosened her grip, smiling gaily. Already, from the corner of her eye, she could see a line of palace attendants with flaming torches creeping up on them.

~

'I give up,' thought Hiranyakashyap after Holika's ashes had been nominally cremated and the thirteen days of official mourning were over. 'Why did the silly woman let herself be burnt in place of Prahlad? Why did she wrap up Prahlad instead and push him into the water the moment they set fire to her?'

Prahlad had had his head ritually shaved and asked to perform Holika's funeral rites himself. Hiranyakashyap had been unable to meet his clear, steady gaze.

'Not a word of reproach,' he wondered. 'The boy hasn't said a word. And I'm his father! We'll see what he has to say tomorrow evening in open court when he's brought in like a prisoner, in chains.'

In the frightened hush of the imperial court next evening, the prince stood in chains by a big pillar near the door. A shaft of fading pink light from outside fell on his composed face. Hiranyakashyap had spent the morning hunting, and had called for a darbar at six in the evening when the torches would be lit and the glittering asura court would look its most magnificent for the crown prince's final trial and sentencing. 'Let all three worlds see and fear my divine justice that does not spare even my son,' thought Hiranyakashyap.

The court commenced with a song of praise for the new god king of the three worlds and after a short, menacing pause Hiranyakashyap began to speak.

'You are all aware of my justice,' he said, and his courtiers barely repressed a shudder. 'You have seen that I do not spare even my son, your crown prince, when he commits the sins of blasphemy and disobedience. I am your lord god and you have seen that I am just. And now you shall see my mercy. The crown prince has been brought before you all because of my mercy. He will be given the chance to publicly disown his heretic belief in the false god, Vishnu, and declare his faith in the true god, me.'

A deathly hush fell upon the court.

Hiranyakashyap got up from his throne and walked majestically down the length of the hall to where Prahlad stood in chains by the pillar near the door. Every eye swivelled to watch his progress, as he knew it would. He had planned it that way so that he could take Prahlad back with him to the throne after the boy's submission.

'Prahlad,' he said, 'admit that you worship a false god

and declare your faith in me, your heavenly father and true god.'

'No, Father, I may not do that. Vishnu is God. I can have no other.'

Hiranyakashyap laughed. 'And where is your fine god to be found? Have you ever seen him or heard him? Do you even know if he exists?'

'Yes, Father, I know he exists. He exists everywhere and in everything.'

'Everything? That's ridiculous. Is he to be found even in this lifeless pillar that you're standing by?' jeered Hiranyakashyap.

'Yes, Father. Even in that very pillar.'

'Such touching faith. Well, call your god out from this pillar, then. I want to see him.'

'Hari, Hari,' said Prahlad calmly and looked at his father, smiling faintly.

A whole minute went by and the very air seemed to sigh.

Hiranyakashyap lost his temper at this anticlimax. 'I'll get your god out for you,' he shouted and kicked the pillar hard.

A second's hush – and the pillar split open with a deafening crack and boom. Screams rent the air as a fearful figure, half lion and half man, emerged with slavering jaws from within the pillar. The towering apparition stepped up to the demon king, picked him up like a doll in its huge, sharp claws and strode to the threshold of the hall.

There on the threshold, neither indoors nor outdoors, in the falling dusk, not by day and not by night, the man-lion, neither a celestial nor an earthling nor a titan, folded one enormous leg into a lap, placed the demon king on it, not on land nor at sea nor in the air, and not by any weapon made, but with its claws, tore open his stomach and disembowelled him.

The man-lion flung away the demon king's corpse and the terrified court shrank as it strode back into the hall to Prahlad and struck off his chains. The crown prince fell to his knees, hands joined in salute. 'My lord Vishnu,' he said, and finally, as never before, not during one of his father's murderous doings, did his young eyes fill with tears and overflow.

The apparition disappeared and in its place shone a column of warm, golden light. A cool, cleansing breeze blew in and the air grew sweet with the scent of night jasmine, of coral-stemmed parijat.

'Be king of your own realm, Prahlad,' said a heavenly voice. 'The celestials and earthlings have their realms back now, and you are the king of Patal. You will make a fine king, staunch soul, and will come to me when it's time.'

Prahlad bent to touch his forehead to the ground. The supernatural light faded and everyone was left looking at Prahlad by torchlight, which had seemed so bright before but now looked feeble after the divine glow that had illumined them.

Prahlad got to his feet and looked around him. He walked with deliberation to the empty throne, sat on it and gazed steadily at his ministers, courtiers, attendants and guards. They looked back at him in awestruck silence. After a few seconds, a shaken cheer broke out and within moments the late demon king's subjects roared in support of their new king in genuine 'excess of joy'. No god this one, thank heaven, but a king. Tomorrow they would cremate his unlamented father. But Prahlad was king now – a boy who had made polite, non-violent non-cooperation his weapon and on whose side was ranged a greater power than ever dreamed of.

12

That Night in Mathura

Janabai was born in the thirteenth century in a central Indian village by the river Godavari in an era of spiritual activism. Abandoned by her starving family when she was seven at the temple of Krishna as Vitthal in Pandharpur, she was rescued and raised in the household of the Marathi poet-saint Namdev. In that atmosphere, often in the company of saints, Jana composed songs that expressed her utter devotion to Vitthal whom she even fondly addressed as 'Arre Kaaltondya', 'O Black-faced One'. Jana was possibly the first Hindu to list the Buddha as the next incarnation of Vishnu after Krishna. Her poems became part of the Vaishnava canon and are still greatly loved. Whatever is known of her life comes from *Bhakta Vijaya*, an eighteenth-century book by the

Marathi writer Mahipati who retold the lives of 108 important saints from the preceding five centuries. The Krishna story had always been retold by male poets and Jana's *Krishna Janma* (The Birth of Krishna) was perhaps its first known telling by a woman. This retelling of the well-known fable is supposedly 'in Jana's voice'.

The dark lord who helps Namdev's maid in her daily chores as if he were her mother, be it washing, sweeping or pounding grain, performs many other tasks as well. No task is too little or too great for him for he himself is smaller than the smallest atom and larger than vast infinity.

He meditated in the heavens before taking his eighth avatar or descent on earth. He put himself through these hardships among us mortals because, as the Preserver, he was sworn to protect the good, punish the wicked and set the world right from age to age.

Krishna was not pleased if asked questions like 'How shall I know you, God? How will I know that it's you?'

'Why do they need to ask? How did they know it was me, the cowherds and milkmaids with whom I lived as a boy before I took the road to Mathura? They knew because they loved me as I loved them. They gave me their hearts as I gave them mine,' he would think. 'Will anyone really understand if I say that I am the unborn, with no beginning or end, the power in everything?'

As Krishna he had chosen to be 'born' in jail.

His earthly mother Princess Devaki and his earthly father Prince Vasudev had laughed and waved from their carriage at the cheering people of Mathura on their wedding day. Devaki's brother Kamsa, king of Mathura, drove them himself through the city to greet the people. But a bodiless voice had silenced them all when it rang through the air to say that Devaki's eighth child would kill Kamsa.

Without another thought, Kamsa had drawn his sword to kill his sister. But her husband, Vasudev, had bravely caught his sword arm. 'It is not your sister's fault, monarch', he had said steadily, holding his bride. 'Take our eighth child, if you must, but do not kill Devaki.'

Kamsa had then locked them up in Mathura jail and each time a child was born to them, he had rushed in and dashed the baby's head against the stone walls, killing it instantly. He had not let one of those seven babies live but had killed them cruelly before their parents' eyes. Poor little mother, poor young father. What cruelty from a brother! Well do the great saints Jnaneshwar and Namdev say that only God is truly kin to us.

How afraid Vasudev and Devaki had been when she

conceived the dreaded eighth child. But as her time drew near, their faces grew pale and calm. They would not let their suffering be in vain. They had clearly been chosen for some task beyond their understanding and they would meet it with courage, whatever it was. The lord would not have let Devaki weep so much for nothing.

Devaki felt sure her child would be born on the eighth night of the moon's dark fortnight in the month of Shravan.

And so it was. There came that glorious hour when the star Rohini arose in the dark night sky and all the planets stood in the best position possible. The stars shone softly, making everything look bright and good while on earth the cities, villages, fields, pasturing grounds and even the underground mines felt a sense of well-being. A great peace fell on the world at that hour.

The rivers sparkled crystal clear and the lakes suddenly bloomed with lotuses although it was night. The birds awoke and chirped softly in joy and swarms of bees buzzed gently in the forests, making pleasant music. The breezes blew sweet scents everywhere, and free of dust, touched tired, sleeping bodies gently, and the oil lamps burned brighter than ever before. The minds of the people who were oppressed by cruel Kamsa and his men grew clear and calm as though they sensed the approaching birth of the Unborn One. Unheard by mortals, the singers in heaven sang sweet songs of welcome in pure, clear voices and the holy men and celestials joined in prayer and showered the finest flowers around them.

Heaving masses of clouds began to fill the sky and move as if in a great dance with the deep, rolling waves of the sea, and all creation seemed to hold its breath when at the darkest hour of the night, Krishna, the world's well-wisher, came forth from the body of Devaki. He appeared among the heartsore and the weary like the full moon rising.

For one dazzling moment Devaki and Vasudev saw their wonderful child stand tall as a god and glow with heavenly radiance. They saw his kind eyes and his four mighty arms that held a conch, a discus, a mace and a perfectly shaped lotus. They saw the divine srivatsa mark on him and the divine jewel Kaustubha around his neck. He wore yellow silk and his body shone darkly beautiful like the rain clouds. He smiled, and his smile held all the compassion in the world. That is how one feels looking at him as Vitthal in Pandharpur.

Overcome by the lord's splendour, Devaki and Vasudev fell at his feet and felt the vision fade. In its place lay a baby with curly dark hair and a face whose beauty made them weep like lost children who suddenly found themselves back home with their mother and father.

A voice told them what to do next. Devaki held her baby the one time, memorizing every feature. The fetters on Vasudev's feet quietly fell away and he gently took the baby from her at the precise moment that Yogmaya, the mysterious force of the Mother Goddess who completes Vishnu, took birth. She was born as a baby daughter to Yashoda, wife of the cowherd Nanda, at Gokul village across the river Yamuna. By Yogmaya's power the guards at the jail and every person in Mathura fell into a deep, dreamless sleep.

The heavy doors of Mathura jail swung open silently for Vasudev, who held Krishna in his arms. He walked out to the river's edge, trying to protect the baby from the rain that suddenly began to pour as he neared the river.

The Yamuna was in full spate and roared and tumbled by with great force, as fiercely as the Godavari in the rains. But when Vasudev, trusting to God's mercy, set his trembling feet in her waters, the great river parted smoothly and made a path for him to cross, just as the ocean yielded to Sita's husband, Ram. However, a wave leapt up to touch the baby's foot for Yamuna could not bear to let him pass without a welcome. As Vasudev stumbled, a dark shadow glided forward and spread its hood above the baby and Vasudev to shelter them from the rain. Intent on crossing carefully, the anxious father hardly noticed that it was the great serpent Adisesha come to serve Vishnu in this new game that the Dark One had begun to play. Are we not all players in his game? Who can blame Yamuna for her impulsive leap? She brims with many memories and surely the sweetest must be of that dark, rainy night in Shravan.

The rain stopped as suddenly as it had begun and Vasudev crossed the river safely, unaware that the great serpent had quietly vanished too. Vasudev found the cowherds' village quite easily. There, as in Mathura, the people lay stone-still in the deep sleep caused by Yogmaya. Vasudeva made his way to the biggest hut, which was that of Nanda, the cowherd chief. He put his son on Yashoda's cot, picked up the newborn baby girl by her side and went back across the now quiet river that let him pass without a murmur to Mathura jail. Yashoda would not suspect a thing when she woke up; she would think it was her child for she had lost consciousness during the birth and now lay like the others under Yogmaya's spell.

The doors of the jail swung open as before and Vasudev made his way undisturbed to Devaki. He placed the baby girl in Devaki's arms and put the fetters back on his feet so that nothing looked out of place.

Devaki stared spellbound at the baby girl's face. Two

dark, bright eyes looked at her with full awareness, blazing with heavenly fire, and Devaki, cradling the tiny body, looked back with the intense love of her starved mother's heart. And then the baby softly dropped her eyelids, for Yogmaya had withdrawn her brilliant gaze out of mercy to the mortal woman. No being on earth had the strength to hold Yogmaya's powerful gaze for even a moment but clean-souled Devaki had been able to exchange that long look with her.

Devaki and Vasudev sat down, leaning against each other, to wait for the morning.

Kamsa would come to wreak his worst. But the world would go on.

The Dark Lord was born and safely away from Mathura.

13

The Touchstone

The touchstone or philosopher's stone called parasmani in Sanskrit and kasauti in Hindi was believed to change iron into gold. It was actually a metaphysical idea. The touchstone symbolized 'spiritual awakening' by which earthly attachment ('iron') was converted to god-love ('gold'). But the possibility of a real touchstone was so alluring and took such firm hold of the collective imagination that many men spent their lives looking for it. This parable about the touchstone is from the *Bhakta Vijaya*, the eighteenth-century Marathi book on the lives and legends of saints. Its special focus is on saints between the thirteenth and seventeenth centuries from the 'Varkari' tradition, centred on Krishna as the deity Vitthal in Pandharpur. Its author, Mahipati, was a scribe-turned-hagiographer. His book was translated into several Indian languages in the last 250 years and into English in the 1920s. Mahipati included a tale about the touchstone to add moral weight to his stories about the poet-saint Namdev. However, it is the tension between the 'earthly' and the 'spiritual' in this medieval fable that may intrigue the modern reader, for some people had reason to feel less than devout.

Having filled her big brass water pot, Kamalaja, wife of the priest Parisa Bhagvat, climbed slowly up the steps of the ghat from the Chandrabhaga. As she reached the top she saw her friend Rajabai arrive on the same errand. Rajabai was the wife of Namdev, son of Gonai and Damaseth the tailor, who had adopted Namdev when they found him floating in the Chandrabhaga as an abandoned baby in a basket. The two friends greeted each other warmly. 'Just wait here while I get the water,' said Rajabai eagerly, longing for a chat, and Kamalaja gladly agreed. She placed her full water pot on the ledge and sat down on the top step to wait for her friend. A pleasant breeze blew by the river and flowering champaka trees on its bank made the air intensely sweet. Kamalaja watched idly as Rajabai filled her pot, kneeling on the last step to do so, and her slow return.

As Kamalaja watched, all kinds of details about Rajabai began to register. Her old earthen pot had a jagged rim against which Rajabai had wadded up a corner of her sari. And what a faded, shabby sari, its edges sadly frayed although it looked washed and clean. Rajabai's face wore a pinched look, her ribcage flashed thin and bony above her waist as she climbed, and she did not wear any jewellery beyond the plainest minimum that a married woman absolutely had to wear. But she'd taken the trouble to put a big red bindi on her forehead and tuck a string of orange aboli flowers in the knot of her hair. 'She's drawing away attention from the fact that she's poor with those bright, happy touches,' thought Kamalaja with a pang of guilt, thinking of her own comfortable life.

Kamalaja felt a strong rush of sympathy. 'God has placed me above want, but not Rajabai,' she thought. 'I must try to help her, somehow.' She waited for Rajabai to reach the top step and went to her as she put her water pot on the ledge and sat down. For a minute or so, the two friends silently watched the broad, curving Chandrabhaga flow by Pandharpur, refreshed by its beauty. Rajabai fetched a deep sigh, which was Kamalaja's cue to begin her investigation.

'You can tell me what the matter is, Rajabai. It's all right to tell a friend. You need not hide it, you know,' she said encouragingly.

Rajabai sighed even more deeply. 'Kamalaja, I feel completely helpless,' she said. 'My husband has forgotten everything because of his obsession with Vitthal. You know his father had a good tailoring business and cloth shop. But he's old now and my husband has no interest in worldly work. He does not care to feed his family. The thatch leaks, there is not enough food in the house, no money to buy more with, no new clothes, not even a new water pot. Besides my parents-in-law, the two of us, our three sons and our maid Jana, we have many guests to feed – just about every holy man who comes to town, I should think. But my husband is so besotted with Rukmini's husband, Krishna, that he does not care that we are ragged and hungry. He is so devoted to the god of the eagle banner that he is deaf to the cries of his own children and to my pleas, his mother's anger and the taunts of the neighbours. I don't pine for finery, Kamalaja, but having been born a human being I do need food, clothes and shelter. It tortures me to see my children hungry. Why did he bring home a wife and beget children on her if he did not mean to look after even their basic needs?'

Kamalaja shook her neatly coiffed head after hearing Rajabai out. 'Is he whom Namdev worships not pleased with him and been generous to him? In that case, why worship him? Why dig in vain if no water is found in a well? If Rukmini's husband won't reward yours, why waste time praising him?'

Rajabai looked so shocked at this worldly wisdom that Kamalaja laughed. 'How you gape! I say so with good reason, you know. Now *my* husband has pleased Rukmini greatly by his prayers and was given a touchstone as his reward. It's our secret. We place a heap of iron filings near it and it turns at once to gold. That's why we are able to eat good food and wear nice clothes and live comfortably. It hurts me to see you in this condition, Rajabai, and hear that your children are hungry. You know I have not been blessed with children. But I try to make the best of things. I'm grateful for my husband and home, which keep me busy and interested at least. What else is allowed to a woman?'

'How lucky you are! It's better not to have children than having to see them miserable. What does a touchstone look like? I've never seen one,' said Rajabai.

'There's nobody at home now, so come with me and I'll show you,' said Kamalaja. The two friends set off to Parisa Bhagvat's house, carrying their water pots. When they got there, Kamalaja insisted that Rajabai first sit down and eat a snack. She rushed to make a hot buttered thalipeeth dal pancake fresh off the griddle that she served Rajabai with a lump of the finest golden jaggery and a delicious portion of cooked tender banana flowers left over from the morning meal. She mixed Rajabai a glass of refreshing taak, making sure to spice the buttermilk with crushed curry leaves.

While Rajabai ate her fill, Kamalaja went to an inner room, opened the big decorated wooden box in which she kept her saris and selected a soft green cotton, not so bright that it would offend Rajabai's family but suitably discreet and pretty that it could be respectably worn by any woman.

'Now see the touchstone,' she said and showed Rajabai the mysterious object that lay hidden in another box. It was just a fist-sized lump of rock and looked completely unremarkable. 'Take it away quickly, wrapped in this sari, which is yours to keep. Let me tie it in a band around your waist,' said Kamalaja fondly. 'Use the touchstone once at home with your own hands; bring iron filings to it yourself. Create a heap of gold to drive away the sorrow of poverty and quickly bring it back. Don't tell your husband, don't tell anybody. I'm certainly not going to tell mine.'

'I'll be free after dinner; I'll bring it back then,' promised Rajabai, greatly touched and pleased. She walked home as fast as she could walk with a heavy water pot and went to her corner. Where could she get iron filings from? There were too many people about;

too many questions would have to be answered. Rajabai looked frantically around. She snatched up her needle, scissors and spinning wheel, all made of iron, and touched them to the magic stone. Gold! They all turned to gold before Rajabai could open her mouth to say 'Deva'. Oh, how kind and good of Kamalaja to have shared her luck.

Rajabai hid away the touchstone with the scissors and spinning wheel and ran to the goldsmith in the bazaar to exchange the golden needle for money. She went straight from the goldsmith to the grocer. 'Send me flour, rice, oil, dal, salt, spices, the best jaggery, coconuts and a good pinch of saffron,' she said breathlessly, handing the grocer some money. 'Keep this against my account. Send everything at once, please!' She dashed away next to buy milk, cream and ghee, and pick out the best vegetables being sold that day.

The grocer's things arrived just as she got home and Rajabai, to the delighted exclamations of her in-laws and her children, began to peel, chop, grate and knead at top speed. Rajabai cooked and cooked and cooked, singing as she worked. She got a splendid meal ready. When it was done, she ran to wash and change into her new sari. She combed her hair and made a new string of flowers for it and waited to welcome her husband.

Namdev came home soon after and Rajabai, glowing with joy, invited him to wash and sit down to dinner. 'I have done my best today to please my family with my skill as a housewife,' she said, beaming.

But Namdev frowned. 'I refuse to eat this. Tell me from where you got the money,' he said sternly and Rajabai was duty-bound to confess. Some sense of impending calamity made her confess only to the golden needle, though.

'Bring me the touchstone,' said Namdev coldly and Rajabai brought it out, silently grieving over her brief, disastrous joy. The food she had cooked with such love and enthusiasm would have to be thrown away now since her husband, the enjoined earthly god for a woman, had rejected it.

She withdrew, scalding tears streaming down her cheeks, as Namdev picked up the touchstone and strode out in fury. He hurled it into the Chandrabhaga and went in waist-deep to bathe.

Meanwhile, Parisa the priest came home and decided to check on the touchstone. Not finding it in its box, he called in his wife, who was embroidering pretty dolls' clothes in silk for the family idols, to demand an explanation.

When Kamalaja shrinkingly confessed to her good deed, Parisa Bhagvat groaned. 'You have ruined us with your foolishness. You have destroyed in a moment what it took a lifetime of prayer to obtain, which other men would kill and die to get. Go now. Bring it back at once from Namdev's house!'

Kamalaja rushed from her large riverside home to Rajabai's small one. 'My husband is home and wants the touchstone returned right now,' she said, panting. 'Please give it back.'

Rajabai whimpered in terror. 'My husband took it away from me. Let's go at once to where he's bathing,' she faltered and they ran anxiously to the riverbank where Namdev was meditating on Vitthal in the middle of his bath. 'Aho, where is Parisa Bhagvat's touchstone?' called Rajabai to his back.

She had to call several times before Namdev turned around, by which time a number of curious people had gathered to watch.

Namdev looked in distaste at the two agitated women.

'I threw it into the river where it belongs,' he said blightingly.

Kamalaja and Rajabai shrieked in horror.

'But it was not yours to throw! It was my husband's. How did you dare?' cried Kamalaja.

'Have you no shame throwing away what was not yours to throw? You have cut my nose off!' wept Rajabai, and both women wailed aloud.

Parisa Bhagvat arrived out of breath just then, driven by anxiety.

The weeping wives turned at once to him and told him what Namdev had done. The crowd stepped closer, not wanting to miss a word.

Parisa Bhagvat began beating his breast and tearing his hair. 'What have you done, you jealous man?' he moaned. 'If you were poor, why did you not ask your Vitthal to bless you? Why did you throw away the touchstone which the goddess gave me? It was not yours to throw!'

The watching crowd began to jeer and chide, 'What jealousy! Poor Kamalaja only meant to help Rajabai feed her hungry children. But this man has destroyed another's wealth through sheer spite. How did he dare throw away what was not his to throw?'

Namdev came out of the water at that, glaring at them all.

'All things belong to Hari and I only returned it to him. You, Parisa Bhagvat! You are called Bhagvat or holy man only because you tell Harikatha at the temple, pleasing the pilgrims at Pandharpur with stories of the lord. And yet you weep and wail as though someone in the family has died because your secret source of wealth has suddenly disappeared. Where are your fine sentiments now, which you uphold at such length in your sermons?

Do you crave an endless supply of gold or do you wish to find the true wealth of a life in the lord through simple living and high thinking?'

'But it was not yours to throw!' cried Kamalaja and Rajabai again furiously.

'Be quiet, women. My question is to Parisa Bhagvat about his touchstone,' said Namdev. 'Now here's a handful of pebbles from the river. Take them, Parisa Bhagvat. Each one of them is a touchstone, I tell you. Test them. Never say that I, Namdev, covet another's wealth. I am rich in the lord, richer than you'll ever be.'

Watched by everyone, Parisa Bhagvat stepped forward and took the stones from Namdev. He looked around for iron objects, and the watching crowd, thinking it a good joke, went up to him one by one and offered whatever iron they had on them – a bangle, an amulet, a trowel tucked into a waistband.

As Parisa touched these objects randomly with one or the other of the pebbles given him by Namdev, each thing turned to shining gold. Cries of joy and amazement filled the air and everybody there rushed to find an iron object to get a share of this wild, unexpected luck.

Finally, when every last person there had obtained something in gold, Namdev looked scornfully at Parisa

Bhagvat. 'Now do you still think I'm jealous of you?' he asked.

Parisa Bhagvat looked at Namdev in utmost wonder, unable to speak.

'You are my master,' he said at last, falling at Namdev's feet. 'Please accept me into your fold and lead me to the lord's lotus feet. I do not need these false touchstones when you, my teacher, can take me to the only wealth worth having.'

He stepped up to the river's edge and flung in the handful of touchstones, every last one of them. They sank at once into the Chandrabhaga, making a fine show of ripples.

A great cheer went up from the crowd for Namdev and Parisa. The two men hugged each other and turned to go to Krishna-Vitthal's temple to offer thanks for the miracle of Parisa's enlightenment and stay on to sing and tell stories in praise of the lord.

The excited crowd followed them, leaving Kamalaja and Rajabai in tears alone by the river, unable to look at each other. Their hearts burned in shame, loss and anger.

~

When the fuss died down, Rajabai secretly sold the scissors and the spinning wheel to the goldsmith and scrupulously gave the money she got for them to Kamalaja to hide away as a nest egg. But though Rajabai was very sad and sorry, she and Kamalaja could never really be friends again. Their mutual affection was soured now by terrible guilt and disappointment.

To prove his godly point, Namdev's god had put an end to the comfort of Parisa's household and taken Kamalaja's husband away from her into Namdev's god-obsessed state of mind. He had ruined Kamalaja's well-meant act of trust and kindness and Rajabai's innocent, lawful pleasure in feeding her family. They were now regarded with no respect at all as two stupid women. Namdev and Parisa were utterly happy in their new-found love for each other and rejoiced all day praising Vitthal in endless discourse. But the light had gone out of their wives' eyes. They had been publicly shown their lowly, worthless place as mere wives, with no rights and no expectations, but only duties.

While Namdev was lost in unworldly contemplation, would his god bathe, dress and feed the three sons that Namdev had begotten on Rajabai's body? Would he buy the grain and cook the food for Namdev's old parents? Oh no, Vitthal managed her husband's world in heaven. It was Rajabai who had to manage her world on earth.

Perhaps her mother-in-law Gonai could have a sharp word with Vitthal? A mother got some respect, a wife, none. But so what if Vitthal did indeed show up at their door one day with food? She, Rajabai, had been publicly shamed for doing just that. Why had she not anticipated her husband's reaction? What if she had lied that some unknown admirer of Namdev's from another region had sent the provisions in respectful homage? That would have convincingly fed his ego and let her feed her children.

Who would lighten lonely Kamalaja's life that she had once contrived to pass busily and happily in devoted companionship with her appreciative husband, keeping her home in perfect order, observing every domestic ritual with refined artistic attention and cooking meal after excellent meal – all for her now-unconcerned god-besotted husband?

Their agonized question to Vitthal remained unanswered as Kamalaja and Rajabai drearily clinked cymbals at yet another musical gathering of saintly men. If he, Rukmini's husband, was indeed the well-wisher of the world, why was he well disposed to only one half of it? How could he live blithely in a palace with Rukmini, enjoying everything while denying mortal Kamalaja and Rajabai the simplest satisfactions of home?

'Perhaps we'll see your famous justice and mercy for

ourselves in another epoch,' they learned to think stoically, 'for you really haven't given us much reason to think well of you in this life, Krishna – unless, we're meant to be deliriously happy with just the fact that our husbands are so drunk on you that they don't drink and beat us?'

14

The Horoscope

Five hundred years ago, Sri Chaitanya Mahaprabhu of Bengal set out to rediscover and map the long-lost physical locations of Vrindavan where Krishna was believed to have played and where the idylls and miracles of his childhood took place. This map is still followed by millions of pilgrims. Sri Chaitanya also conjured an inner landscape, of a life absorbed in thoughts of Krishna, which he called the 'hidden treasure of the Vrindavan within'. He urged that the path to the treasure lay in the practice of Naam, in repeating Krishna's names, particularly the refrain 'Hare Rama, Hare Krishna' and in singing kirtan, songs in Krishna's praise. Chaitanya Mahaprabhu travelled across the country to a number of holy places to spread his gospel of Krishna worship

> and met and debated with other religious personalities of the day, attracting many followers. He taught his disciples how to find their way to the 'hidden treasure' of Krishna love in their own minds through parables like this one, which he is said to have narrated to his disciple Sanatana Goswami.

Sarvajna, whose name means 'all-knowing', was indeed omniscient but he took care not to reveal it. He was trained in mathematics, astronomy and astrology at Ujjain, the city that was considered particularly well acquainted with time and space. Time itself was said to have begun at Ujjain, and the prime meridian of the old universe of discourse passed through it. The lunar calendar or panchang was cast at Ujjain and every festival, every moonrise and sunset, every twelve-yearly Kumbh Mela was calculated to the tick of the dot. The calendar itself, the Vikram Samvat or era of King Vikramaditya, had been created in Ujjain and it had once been home to legendary mathematicians-astronomers-astrologers Varahamihira and Bhaskara the Second.

Sarvajna belonged to this elite university of minds and was not afraid of his own powers. The reason for this inner serenity and outward composure was simple. Sarvajna had true perspective, which made him an intensely private person. The time was rife with quarrels between competing schools of thought on just about everything, from science to astronomy to medicine to religion. Sarvajna, despite his formidable scholarship, refused to be drawn into these arguments, especially about religion. He considered his almost miraculous powers a gift from god, no more and no less. He understood that he was meant to use them to help floundering humanity. So he kept a very low profile and never showed off. Nor did he encourage the rich and famous to visit him or invite him home for then he would be caught in their toils. However, he was non-judgemental and maintained friendly ties. Sometimes, when he found that they were inclined to philanthropy, he dropped his guard a little and let fall a gentle hint about genuinely deserving recipients.

Sarvajna's active mind lived in an active body. He was fond of walking through the countryside from village to village, discovering the land and its people on his way to a great temple or to visit a fellow scholar. On one such foray, he took a slightly different path and stopped at a prosperous-looking village for a short rest. As he looked about him, a thin, shabby young man caught his eye. With his great powers of observation and insight, Sarvajna sensed a mystery about the young man. He signalled to him to come over. He was not mistaken in these matters.

The shabby young man surprised him, however, by greeting him very respectfully as 'acharya', or 'teacher'.

'How do you know that, son?' asked Sarvajna.

'You have the look of a distinguished scholar, sir,' said the young man, whose name was revealed to be Nalin.

'You speak like a person of birth and education, my boy. I would like to see your horoscope,' said Sarvajna with delicacy, wanting to know more.

'I was born to a good home, sir, and a fine family. But I am destitute now, I almost beg for a living,' said the young man matter-of-factly. 'Please wait, I'll fetch my horoscope.' He darted into the temple nearby, spoke to the priest and came out in a minute or so with a painted box in which lay his horoscope.

'I left it for safekeeping with the priest,' he explained but Sarvajna did not hear him for he had already extracted the palm leaves and was casting a keen, deductive eye on them. The young man watched him intently.

'But I don't understand!' exclaimed the master astrologer, looking up suddenly. 'Why are you destitute? I can see from your chart that your father has left you a great fortune. However, I also see that he could not tell you where he concealed it because he died in a foreign land while out trading. All you have to do is find your treasure and live happily ever after.'

'How do I do that, sir? I wouldn't know where to begin,' said the young man who had brightened for a moment but looked downcast again. 'I live in a small corner of my huge old family house. There is no one left but me and I am unfit for anything, having been brought up as the spoilt son of the house when my father was alive. All I can do is earn a few coins copying manuscripts for the priest and hiring myself out as an occasional letter writer. I can barely manage to feed myself with what I earn, let alone afford quills and ink.'

'Well, you are an honest lad,' said Sarvajna, appreciating Nalin's frank and clinical description of his plight. It was a refreshing change from the weepers and wailers and he felt that this unusual boy deserved his best effort. 'Let me think,' said Sarvajna and began to breathe deeply and meditate, gradually cutting off all sounds and sensations until he withdrew far into the grove of his thoughts where there was only light and a cool, sweet breeze, and if he listened hard enough, the faint sound of a magic flute.

When he had withdrawn into the deepest recess of his mind and asked humbly for guidance, Sarvajna was suddenly blessed with a revelation of the eighth verse from the tenth canto of the Song of God. 'I am the infinite treasure, worship me with love and discover my richness. The Vedas and all schools of thought and all forms of worship are but my creation. Find me,' said the revelation.

A greater riddle had been unexpectedly solved for him.

'We live in confusing times and are unable to realize our soul connection with god,' thought Sarvajna soberly when he emerged from the trance. 'The south country is overly ritualistic and a seeker will be stung by the poison of its pointless arcania. The north is like an enormous serpent waiting to swallow a seeker whole. It is full of trickster yogis pretending to be gurus who mislead the public into excesses of false fervour. The west is like a land of ghosts; it is emotionally barren, being given over to endless academic wrangles that discard god. The east, which is the natural source of light for the sun rises there, represents pure god-love free of rituals, tricks and dry argument. That is the path of Krishna and the meaning of the revelation. I see it clearly now. Nor do the stars lie to me. I think I have also found the solution to this young man's problem.'

Opening his eyes, Sarvajna smiled affectionately at Nalin.

'If you would care to take my advice, son, let us collect some labourers and spades and I will tell you where to dig.'

They set off soon in an excited party for Nalin's ancestral house and Sarvajna issued crisp, precise orders.

'Leave the southern, northern and western sides be.

Let us focus on the eastern side of your home, where the light lives,' he said and surveyed that part of the house. The entrance was in the northeast, as prescribed by the rules of house-building. 'Here, to the right, I think,' said Sarvajna, pointing to where a fine shiuli tree bloomed near the once-grand front door. It had evidently been planted there so that every guest who approached the house when it bloomed to herald the festival of Navratri would pass through a cloud of scent past a carpet of flowers.

'Dig here without damaging the root,' said Sarvajna, pointing to the base of the shiuli.

After about an hour of steady, careful digging by the two hired workers, Sarvajna and Nalin heard the sound they were waiting for, a loud clunk as the spade hit an iron chest. The heavy box was hauled up, dusted off and tenderly deposited in an inner room of the house. The labourers refilled the hole and it was Sarvajna who paid them for Nalin had no money.

After the labourers left, Nalin broke the locks on the box with a hammer and almost fell down in shock when he lifted the lid. Not only was the treasure chest most satisfyingly packed with solid gold ingots, but there was also a sturdy bag of thick silk laid on top that was found to contain handfuls of Burmese rubies and Sri Lankan sapphires and a most unusual pearl necklace assembled from rare and precious pearls of all shapes and shades from all the seven seas.

Nalin fell at Sarvajna's feet and thanked him profusely.

'My blessings, Nalin. I know already that you will do well and prosper.' Sarvajna smiled, pleased at the happy outcome of the sudden hunch that had visited him when he saw Nalin. 'Well, I must be off now. I will be back, you know, to demand my fee – that you help other people along in the world.'

'I thought there was more to what you told me, Teacher, besides the location of my father's treasure,' said Nalin with glad respect. 'Please come again when I have set my house in order so that I may learn of those other treasures from you.'

15

The Impersonator

Sri Ramakrishna Paramahamsa (1836–86), who left a deep influence on modern Hindu life, would often speak to his followers on the power of associating with anything holy. He was strongly of the opinion that such an association would transform a person's character and behaviour for the better, and he explained this view through many parables. One such story involved the folk art of 'bohurupi', meaning 'many forms'. The bohurupi was a professional impersonator who disguised himself as a god or goddess or another mythological character, or as a bird, animal or character from real life which was easily recognizable by the costumes and stories. He was a one-man show, responsible for everything about his performance from costume to dialogue. Bohurupis were once in great demand in rural and urban Bengal for lack of other entertainment. They performed in return for food, clothes or money, constantly travelling from place to place and to religious fairs and festivals. This brief parable by Sri Ramakrishna is retold to convey the saint's message along with a glimpse of the old bohurupi life and the jatra or traditional theatre that it came from.

Jogen, being a lowly bohurupi or itinerant impersonator of mythological roles, could not afford a horse carriage to the riverside like the rich merchants, landed aristocrats and employees of the British administration. He walked ten miles to the wharf from the last village he had performed at, and took the cheapest ferry across the river to the island. Once across, he trudged up to the great Vaishnava temple. Its presiding deity was the sixteenth-century saint Sri Chaitanya Mahaprabhu, considered the earthly embodiment of Krishna himself, and by some even greater than the Dark Lord. Jogen arrived in time for one of the free handouts of chopped fruit, rice and sweets served to the poor by a rich devotee, which pleased him greatly. It felt like a personal welcome from Chaitanya Mahaprabhu who had been born three hundred years before Jogen's entirely unremarkable arrival on earth. Chaitanya, who had rekindled the love of Krishna in thousands of hearts and rediscovered all the lost holy sites of Krishna's childhood in Vrindavan, was in a sense Jogen's personal patron saint.

It was Chaitanya who had famously added new lustre to the jatra, the old travelling folk theatre of the land. Chaitanya had preached the equality and brotherhood of all men whatever their caste and thrown himself into religious ecstasy as he sang and danced to Krishna in the streets of Nabadwip with his followers. One memorable day, he had told his disciple Chandrasekhar that he wished to perform the play *Rukmini Haran*. This famous love story described how Krishna stole away Princess Rukmini of Chedi after he received her desperate love letter asking him to rescue her from being married to someone else. Chaitanya had wanted the costumes, make-up and jewellery to be perfect. He had played the role of Princess Rukmini, transforming himself so completely that nobody could make out that it was their guru. The performance had gone on through the night at Chandrasekhar's house and ended only in the morning. Was there anybody in the land from the high Himalayas to the far western desert to the seashores of the far south who did not know the story?

This was the beautiful ideal that had spread through the land, of emotionally investing yourself so deeply in a role while you did your make-up and put on your vesha or costume that you entered the spirit of the character you were going to depict. A profound sense of vesha descended on Jogen each time he played a role. He thought over what he went through each time he prepared for a role, trying to enter the personality of the character he was going to depict. He took on the character's smallest likely mannerisms and tried to connect with the character's inner spirit as he took on the outer appearance layer by layer. Last of all, before he placed the character's wig or crown on his head, he shut his eyes and prayed deeply that the character should live in him during his enactment. The actor who could do that created an energy field that invited the audience to enter and share his feelings. And what was the purpose of the play except to make people really feel something – feel cleansed, inspired and renewed to get on with everyday life after the show? 'God is the greatest Actor of all who makes each one of us perform in his divine comedy and Chaitanya Mahaprabhu was god on earth,' thought Jogen adoringly as he prostrated at the temple.

A family of six went past him, its two little sons jostling each other playfully. Jogen remembered his elder brother with a pang as he often did these days. Their father, the priest of the small Kali temple in their village, had been intensely devout. Jogen's elder brother had succeeded to his father's duties and wanted Jogen, who had a knack for languages and music, to start a small village school to add to the family income. But Jogen had deserted the green paddy fields, coconut groves and lotus-filled ponds of his village. He had given his heart to the magic of the jatra troupes that came by each year during the big festivals to perform for the landlord of his village. The landlord would set up a separate camp and kitchen for the actors and everyone was invited to watch a full week of plays that usually began in the afternoon and went on till sunrise. The pala or jatra plays were a mixture of prose, verse and song, especially song. A jatra play had as many as fifty songs, and the landlord was partial to the eighteenth-century musical drama *Bidya Sundar*, a historical romance.

Jogen knew that his brother did not quite approve of melodrama and scenes of abduction and gory, demonic deaths. But ever since the land settlements made by the East India Company after they became the owners of all Bengal had made a number of local people rich, the new landed gentry had set out to be patrons of theatre and regularly invited jatra troupes to their fiefs.

Jogen found the love legends, mythological episodes, historical romances and tales of robbers and saints thrilling, as indeed did everyone else in the village except his excessively saintly brother. After one scolding too many from his brother and one taunt too much from his brother's wife about hangers-on who did not work but only watched plays, Jogen had run away.

He had left overnight with a visiting jatra troupe and never gone home again. The troupe had accepted him because of his fine speaking and singing voice and his obvious passion for the actor's craft. Jogen had worked his way up the roles – from playing a servant, a gardener, an attendant or a junior demon, he graduated to increasingly bigger roles until he was allowed to play the gods. Some of the troupe's senior actors preferred playing Krishna and Durga so Jogen was often cast as Shiva. Shiva had given the world its music with the first syllable, 'Om', and Shiva was the divine dancer whose energy kept the world moving. To better enter the spirit of Shiva, Jogen learned to play the musical instruments that accompanied a jatra play, for what was jatra without music? Indeed, it was called jatra-gaan or jatra-song by the people and when they went to watch a play they did not say they were going to watch it, they said they were going to hear it, as one did a concert.

Accordingly, Jogen had learned to play the pakhawaj and dholak and the violin-like behala, and became fairly adept at singing classical ragas like Yaman and Bhairavi. But he had found himself deeply drawn to the simple, primeval damru, the hand drum of Shiva that was an indispensable prop for that role, along with the three-pronged trishul, the tiger skin around the waist, the wig of matted hair, the stuffed cloth snake around the neck, ashes on the body and a third eye painted on the forehead with lamp black and red aalta paint.

More and more, Jogen had wandered away to play the damru by himself and dance as Shiva must have danced his tandava. He had trained with village wrestlers to build his body and practised his role endlessly in *Amritarpan*, the episode in which devas and asuras churned the ocean of milk to bring forth the elixir of life hidden in its depths. But before that the ocean had expelled a terrible, world-destroying poison. Shiva had drunk poison to save the world. Jogen felt his eyes smart with tears. Was there ever such an unselfish god, moreover one who disdained finery and lived so simply? While people dressed up every other god and goddess as if they were babies, kings and queens, nobody dared play around with Shiva, no, not one frill did they dare festoon him with. A role of roles, indeed, and Jogen always lit an earthen lamp with oil in it while he dressed as Shiva and prayed to it before and after he put on his vesha. Sometimes, when he had to perform after a long, tiring walk, he smoked a pipe of weed to take the edge off his fatigue and help him concentrate.

By and by, Jogen had not wanted to play any other role and been expelled by the troupe, which had no room for ultra-specialists. He had had to become a bohurupi then, a wandering solo impersonator who went from village to village playing a goddess one day, a tiger or a monkey the next and Krishna or Shiva the third. While Jogen's free spirit rejoiced that he was not imprisoned in a classroom teaching grammar and mathematics in a village school, the song of the open road was not always tuneful. For instance, he could not perform on Thursdays because on that day every householder worshipped Lakshmi, the goddess of good fortune, and did not part with money, rice or potatoes for that would have been like handing away the luck the goddess had supposedly blessed them with that day.

Sometimes a village was so intensely Vaishnava that it did not tolerate the sight of any other deity. Despite his artistic immersion in Shiva's role, Jogen loved Krishna as ardently as Shiva on the principle that god was one. This solid precept had been drilled into him by his father and brother and he had neither an intellectual nor an emotional reason to quarrel with it. So he had to leave villages that were the exclusive domain of Thakur, Lord Krishna…

~

The little family that had made him long to see his brother again had finished its rounds and offered worship and they went past Jogen again. They looked like a devout, god-loving lot and were dressed in fine muslin and silk. The mother and daughters wore a fair amount of gold and the little boys had a thick gold chain each around their necks. Jogen felt sure they would prove to be good patrons. He stood up and saluted the father politely. 'I would be glad to perform for you, sir, I am a bohurupi,' he offered.

The family stopped and considered him gravely.

After a moment, the father nodded. 'My estate is at Lakshmiganj,' he said pleasantly, naming a village some distance away on the mainland. 'We have to go now but you are welcome to perform at our village if it's in your direction.'

'I would like that,' said Jogen and the landlord looked again at him for Jogen's shabby appearance and cultured accent were a curious contrast.

'Do you prefer a particular theme?' asked Jogen.

'It will be Shivratri in a few days, so perhaps you might like to present something about Shiva,' said the man.

Jogen's eyes lit up. 'I should like that very much indeed,' he said happily. The landlord gave him directions and left with his family.

~

Jogen arrived a few days later at the landlord's village and went to pay his respects at the local temple first to Shiva and Kali. It brought back vivid memories of home as other temples in his wandering life had not and he was especially respectful in his greetings to the priest, who in turn spoke kindly and invited him home to wash and rest. He nodded approvingly over lunch when Jogen explained the reason for his visit to the village and offered to escort him to the landlord's estate.

The landlord was pleased to see Jogen and after he had told them about his background and repertoire, a plan was made to have Jogen perform a panchali or solo of Shivlila, the idylls of the great god. They decided to have the performance in the open ground next to the temple where all could gather and hear; the village men and boys on three sides and the women on the fourth.

Since it was a solo, Jogen would perform on the ground and not require a wooden stage raised two feet high with a ramp as a proper jatra would.

'I'm only a lowly bohurupi after all; it is quite a bit of luck to get so much respect and attention from these people,' thought Jogen as he was led away after the meeting by the landlord's servant to quarters at the back.

He assembled his kit from the cloth bag in which he carried his costumes and make-up and spent the afternoon repairing a dent in his trishul, mending a small tear in the printed length of chintz that served as his tiger skin and finding empty coconut shells in the backyard to mix paints in. The landlord's cook lent Jogen his daughter's mirror for Jogen's own tiny one was unaccountably missing.

When it was time to perform, Jogen made his way in full costume to the temple and stood waiting for his audience, his body tilted slightly forward. Oil lamps had been lit and tall flaring torches had been planted at the four corners of the space he was to perform in.

The villagers assembled excitedly, chattering and laughing, the gold-covered iron bangles of the married women clinking as they happily took their appointed places. The priest sat in front and raised wooden seats covered with mats, cushions and bolsters awaited the landlord and his family, who soon arrived to occupy them.

It was time.

As he sang his prelude and opening invocation, Jogen felt something stir deep in his heart like it never had before. He forgot everything and everybody as he began to enact the thrilling deeds of the Mahayogi Shiva, who was so many things to so many people. The ultimate sanyasi but also the head of the First Family; the husband whose deeds always surprised his wife, Goddess Parvati, for there was no telling what he would do next; the tender father of Ganesha and Kartikeya. Indeed, Shiva and Parvati were the father and mother of the universe; but the great god was so happy with so little that they called him 'asutoshi', 'easily pleased'; he was very slow to anger but if someone crossed the line there was no telling how Shiva's fury would erupt, whether as fire from his third eye or as a dance of destruction. And yet, everybody loved to love him for he was complex, interesting, endearing, terrifying, remote and reachable all at once. Was there ever such a god to keep those who loved him so awestruck, delighted and grateful?

Jogen hardly heard the sobs, sighs, laughter and wild applause as he sang, danced, acted and recited the Shivlila for four hours without a break. Nor could anyone stir, watching him. He felt uplifted and exhilarated and sensed great waves of intense energy coming at him from the audience as mood chased mood.

When it ended, nobody could say a word at first. And then, what a roaring, stamping and happy outcry from the crowd as the landlord, tears pouring down his face, took off his pearl necklace and offered it to Jogen.

But what was this?

Jogen shook his head, raised his arms in salute and walked away. The landlord shrugged in surprise and the startled crowd began to disperse as Jogen slipped away to his quarters, washed off his paint, put away his costume and dropped into a deep, exhausted sleep without eating his dinner.

The next morning, as the landlord drank his tea on the broad, pillared verandah of his lordly house, the attendant led Jogen in, his cloth bag on his shoulder, evidently ready to take to the road again.

After greetings were exchanged, and compliments and thanks, Jogen said, 'Please would Your Honour give me the pearl necklace you so kindly wanted to bestow on me last night?'

'Why, certainly!' exclaimed the landlord in surprise. 'But why do you want it now?'

'I am going back to my village, sir,' said Jogen. 'I'm going home to my brother. With the money from your necklace, I will start a village school and repay my debt to my brother and also do my share of work in the world.'

'I commend you on your decision,' said the landlord, taken aback but pleasantly so. He considered Jogen seriously. 'You are an immensely gifted artiste. But our world is changing every day now with new inventions and discoveries from overseas. We must be prepared for it and education is the only thing that will prepare us. Please wait, I will fetch it myself.'

He came back with the pearl necklace in a blue velvet pouch and two more bags; one full of silver coins and a small one with five golden English guineas in it.

'This should last your school a long time, please take it,' he said, smiling, and Jogen, scarcely believing his luck, did so with many grateful words and took formal leave.

'Just one thing,' said the landlord, curious, as Jogen turned to go. 'Why did you refuse it last night?'

'Your Honour, how could I take it then? I was Shiva last night and the great god does not accept money or valuables,' said Jogen and left quietly. He knew he would never act again after the divine exhilaration he had felt the previous night. He could not bear the idea of playing Shiva or any another role now and possibly experience anything less and his heart had been telling him to go home for weeks. It was best this way – a brilliant, glowing memory to keep all his life.

The landlord was left shaking his head in pleased surprise. 'We may be on the brink of all kinds of changes. But I suspect the gods won't let us forget them,' he thought. 'Anyhow, I need not worry that he'll waste my money. If he's off to be a schoolteacher, I know he will totally be one.'

16

The Dancing Girl

Swami Vivekananda (1863–1902), the spiritual successor to Sri Ramakrishna Paramahamsa, was the founder of the Ramakrishna Mission and its monastic order of scholarship and service. He went on a tour of the Himalayan foothills and to Kashmir in 1893 with a party of friends and followers, which included his American disciple Sister Nivedita. She kept a diary of the tour and noted that when the swami and friends stopped by the lake town of Naini Tal, a popular holiday resort, they were invited to dinner one evening by the Raja of Khetri, who greatly admired Vivekananda. The swami came to know that the raja had invited a dancing girl to perform for them. Being a monk, he disliked the plan but went along out of politeness. However, the dancing girl came to know of the swami's objection and presented a spiritual song by the medieval poet Surdas. What happened next was like an 'action replay' of the old tale from the Mahabharata about the butcher and the brahmin: when he heard the unmistakably high-souled content of the dancing girl's song, the swami was greatly struck and realized that one had to look beyond a person's profession to their nature and character. A parable that he shared on a later occasion recalls that poignant real-life encounter.

Not far from Mathura and Vrindavan on the banks of the Yamuna was a little village whose chief claim to anything was that it lay not far from the king's highway. Pilgrim parties and wandering minstrels did not know of it nor would they have cared, had they known, to cross the fields and mango groves beyond which it was hidden, barely a couple of kilometres from the highway. But any number of travelling salesmen and traders from other towns who had business in Mathura and Vrindavan would look forward on their way back, when their business was done and they were homeward bound with money in their saddlebags or in their high-domed bullock carts, to a pleasant little detour by that village.

Nobody ever spoke of it but the visitors always left

some of their money behind in the village. Not only were sweets and snacks required sometimes but betel leaves and areca nuts and pitchers of milk, pots of curds and the occasional services of the blacksmith, cobbler and tailor. The visitors always went straight to the headman's house to pay him their respects. They sat with him on string cots under the big neem tree in his outer courtyard and gave him small gifts and news of the world. By and by, after a polite half-hour of chit-chat, they would announce their intention of going for 'a walk by the river' and the headman would bid them a cordial goodbye at his back door. He never had to say 'Do come by again soon' even for form's sake for it was clearly understood that they would.

A small path led from behind the headman's house to the riverside. This spared visitors and villagers a public parade down the main street of the village past the homes and shops of respectable folk and their innocent children playing at hoops and tops and hopscotch. Instead, the travelling salesmen and merchants went jauntily down the path at the back through a small copse of jamun trees to the riverside. There in the shade of a fine kadamba tree stood a trim little cottage of lime-washed mud with a thatched roof and a brick-and-stucco sit-out. In it lived an attractive lady of not more than twenty summers who waited to receive them with a welcoming smile. The visitors never stayed long unless they planned to have lunch while the blacksmith, cobbler or tailor attended to minor repairs to their conveyance that they had left at the headman's front door, in which case the food arrived, already paid for by the visitors.

They always left smiling but the lady of the house never came to her door to see them off. Every day without fail, songs and the sounds of anklets on dancing feet could be heard from the little house. Once a month, and always at Janmashtami, Krishna's birthday festival, the lady would make her way beautifully dressed to the village temple and offer the Blue God her art in nritya seva or worship through dance. She lived very quietly otherwise except for her visitors, who were never heard to make a noise either. No noisy vulgar revels or brawls ever disturbed the riverside because of them.

The young lady was a dancing girl from Mathura, the daughter of a dancing girl who had been the daughter of a dancing girl and so on, going back a hundred generations. But her father had been the village priest with no children by his legal wife who had died of a miscarriage. All his paternal feelings were invested in this daughter, the chance result of a youthful indiscretion. He had taught her her prayers himself, delighting in her affectionate ways on his discreet twice-yearly visits to see her before New Year and Deepavali, when it was a father's pleasant duty to give his child gifts. When he fell ill and thought he would soon be gone, he had asked the headman to let his daughter, whose mother was recently dead, to live in the village and let her earn her living in the only way she could.

'She is alone in the world and without money. She would be torn to pieces in no time at all in the city in her trade. Nor will she escape if she hires herself out as a maid to avoid her mother's life. I cannot bear to think of her slaving in some ill-tempered or lecherous person's house. Where else may she go but to her father's village? She may be a dancing girl and not acceptable on the main street. But what if she could live quietly out of sight by the river? Her mother's friends in town will tell only a few trusted people about her and describe her attractively as a novelty, as private entertainment away from spies and witnesses. And once these visitors see her, I am certain they will want to come back. Her income will be assured. I know this is most irregular but I assure you that her nature is soft and god-loving. She won't give you any trouble. You know I have no one to whom I can entrust responsibility. Please let her live safely in your midst, it would give my soul peace,' the priest had begged with tears in his eyes.

The headman had put it to vote quietly with the men of the village and though startled at first, nobody really had an objection. They were moved by their priest's agony as a father and began to feel protective of his daughter themselves. Dancing girls were part of society like anyone else and though they had never seen her, she was indisputably a daughter of the village and her father was greatly liked and had served the village well. As long as she lived quietly and kept away from their children, they did not mind. Nor would they trouble her themselves or gossip about her or object if she had visitors from elsewhere. Yes, she could come to the temple and they would make their mothers and wives understand that an orphan daughter of the village, though a dancing girl, deserved their protection.

And so Punita, for that was the name chosen for her by her father, had come to live in the village and become the best-kept secret on the king's highway. She was pretty without being outrageously beautiful, dressed modestly and spoke politely. Even the wives, aunts and grandmothers had no real problem for she was indeed very gentle and her once-yearly dance at the temple had a sincerity and grace that touched their hearts and made them think well of her and sympathize deep down, though outwardly they pretended not to notice when she handed fruits and flowers to the new priest to offer to god.

Only one person in the village disliked Punita and made no secret of it. This was the resident sanyasi who most unfortunately for him had settled down near the river before Punita came to stay. The sanyasi had a clear view of Punita's house and the comings and goings of the travelling salesmen and the shopkeepers. His meditations were disturbed by the sound of her anklets and though her songs were always about Krishna and never vulgar, they infuriated him because she was not a respectable housewife but a single working woman. He did not stop to consider that Punita had had no choice in her occupation and that it was really no different from being a priest, a merchant, a farmer or a potter. Used to living on alms, he had no appreciation of those who worked at hard and often unpleasant jobs for sheer survival. He lived on milk, fruit and yoga, and singing and dancing seemed a wicked way of life to him compared to what he did, which was to deliver a weekly evening discourse on god and godliness at the temple.

Nityanand, for that was the sanyasi's name, meaning 'eternal joy', made it his cause in life to harangue and scold Punita every single day. 'A wicked woman like you, leading a wicked life, is sure to go to hell. Mend your ways, think of god and beg his forgiveness!' he told her unfailingly and spent his days simmering in anger and monitoring the comings and goings at Punita's house, noting what songs she sang, how long she danced and what she wore when she went to the temple. He completely failed to see that his own weekly discourses were held at the very temple where Punita danced in praise of the very same god. Instead, his speeches began to include stern warnings of hellfire and damnation for sinners and every year after Punita's dance at the temple, he would march up to the headman's house and tick him off for permitting, in fact aiding and abetting, such goings-on.

'I shall complain to the authorities at Mathura,' he once warned in a temper.

The headman merely cracked his knuckles and called Nityanand's bluff with a few unpleasant truths.

'Do that. And please stay on in Mathura, you need not come back,' he said witheringly. 'Punita belongs to this village. You don't. You just came along one day and decided to stay on and live on our charity whereas she earns her living and helps others in the village earn something, too. She is a polite, god-loving girl. It is her bad luck that her birth prevents her from making a respectable marriage and living a normal life like other women. But in the view of this village, she is more "normal" and better behaved than many so-called respectable people. We made a pact among ourselves to let her live in peace, at first for her dead father's sake and then for her own when we saw her for ourselves. Don't you recognize character when you see it?'

'You will all burn in hell with her, sinners,' cried the sanyasi and returned to his tree in a rage, knowing that he lacked the guts to leave his safe perch in the village and take to the path, trusting to the charity of strangers like a sanyasi was actually supposed to. He took out his fury on Punita the next morning, threatening her with the most hideous punishments in the afterlife, reducing her to tears.

Twenty years passed by in this harsh, unrelenting manner. The sanyasi grew ever crankier and as Punita grew older too and began to lose her youthful looks, the number of visitors began to decline. Already fond of prayer and holy songs, she spent more and more of her time thinking of god and was able to live thriftily on her savings. She and her hostile neighbour eventually died within barely a day of each other.

~

Punita and Nityanand waited as bodiless pretas in the ether for their death ceremonies to be completed on earth after which they would know their fate in the afterlife. In that in-between state, as spirits still attached to earth, they hoped and prayed to be taken to god's feet for good and never come back. But two very different troops of beings arrived and seized them. A group of ghouls bound the sanyasi and began to drag him towards the netherworld while a band of heavenly beings affectionately took the dancing girl's hand and led her upwards to the light.

'Wait!' cried the sanyasi. 'Why am I, a holy man who spoke of holy things, being taken to hell while that evil woman, despite her sinful life, is obviously going to heaven?'

The ghouls cackled evilly and prodded the angry sanyasi with their long nails. The angels stopped and turned their sweet faces to look pityingly at him.

Finally, an angel spoke.

'You may have been a sanyasi but you were obsessed with evil. You spent most of your time thinking hateful thoughts about this woman. Whereas she, though forced to live the life she did because she had no earthly choice, had her mind fixed on god and tried her best to think good thoughts. We become what we think, sanyasi. Her mind is far cleaner than yours and so therefore is her soul. That is why she goes with us to the light. But you, because you thought of sin all the time and always spoke cruel words, must go join the sinners.'

The sanyasi had no answer to that and hung his head in shame while the angels and the dancing girl, casting him a compassionate look, turned their faces to the light and disappeared into it.

17

The Voice in the Woods

Sri Ramakrishna Paramahamsa (1836–86) told many brief but deeply symbolic parables to convey his messages of spiritual guidance. In one such story, Sri Ramakrishna tells of a child called Jatila – which was a popular name for both girls and boys and can be taken to mean 'everyone' – who is afraid to cross the deep, dark woods ('life') to get to school ('knowledge' as in 'spiritual realization'). This nineteenth-century parable by Sri Ramakrishna was retold as a charming child's story by Swami Vivekananda's American disciple Margaret Noble or Sister Nivedita. It appeared as the tale 'Gopala and the Cowherd' in her book *Cradle Tales of Hinduism* in 1907. It was presented in that form as an illustrated story by Amar Chitra Katha and continued to be retold as a delightful tale for children through the twentieth century.

While the 'Gopala' version may be well known and easily available today, Sri Ramakrishna's original parable is somewhat lost and forgotten. It is expanded and retold here for modern readers in the new millennium in an attempt to convey the saint's telling of this symbolic tale.

Jatila lived in a village across the forest from his school. School was excellent fun but going home in the late afternoon through the dark, shadowy forest frightened Jatila. He was only eight and had just begun to go to school as little boys did at that age. But he did not like to own that he was afraid to his schoolmates because his name meant 'lion'. He was meant to be brave. He had not quite grown into his name; that was all.

'I won't be so afraid next year when I'll be older and more used to it, or the year after that,' he thought sturdily as he marched along the narrow jungle path between the trees. 'I'm only afraid because I'm so little now and don't know how to fight or talk in a bold, loud voice like the big boys can.'

'Phee-yeaan,' screeched a wild peacock suddenly, somewhere close in the jungle, making Jatila jump in fear. 'It's just a silly old peacock. It startled me,' he told himself stoutly, his heart thumping a little. But the next minute the sudden rustle of an animal breaking cover behind him made Jatila scream. It was only a jackal but its teeth were very sharp and its eyes gleamed red in the rays of the setting sun that streaked through the forest. Jatila broke into a desperate run down the jungle path.

When he got home, gasping, he saw a group of women sitting around his mother, who was telling them a story about Vishnu. Of course, it was the fourth Friday of the month. His mother was both weaver and storyteller to the women of their village. That's how she was able to keep the thatch over their heads and pay the schoolmaster's fee and pay the hired hands to harvest the belt of mango trees behind their cottage or do the heavy digging for the vegetable garden or repair the little wooden cowshed in which their only cow lived. But his mother did not choose to pay anyone to escort him to school.

'Men can be more dangerous than animals, Jatila,' she had said, her face very stern. 'You must grow up soon, I'm afraid.'

Jatila's father had died of a fever just three months after Jatila's eighth birthday, when he had barely received his sacred thread. Since he had had his initiation ceremony,

Jatila was considered technically grown-up from the ritual point of view even though he was only eight. He had had to light his father's funeral pyre himself and go through the entire thirteen days of rituals guided by the village priest. His newly widowed mother had been silent and withdrawn through it all, barely noticing whether Jatila ate or drank or slept.

'Who will look after us now, Mother?' he'd asked after the thirteen dreadful days were over. 'Will we have enough to eat and drink now that Father's dead?'

'We have enough, and I will earn more with my spinning and weaving. I'm the best weaver in five villages around, Jatila,' said his mother, a flash of fire suddenly appearing in her eyes. 'And I also get ghee, fruit, rice and clothes as offerings when I tell the village women the Harikatha every month.'

'I wish I had a brother or sister, Mother,' said Jatila, leaning on his mother's shoulder.

'You have noticed our biggest problem, Jatila,' sighed his mother, holding him close. 'We are not poor in the sense of not having things to eat and drink or a roof over our heads. But we are very poor in people. We don't have a single person to really call our own. The village is very good to us, of course. But at the end of the day, it's just you and me, son.'

She laughed suddenly, a short, unamused laugh. 'And god, of course.'

'You know god well, don't you, Mother? You tell his stories every month and you pray every day,' said Jatila. His mother laughed that strange laugh again.

'Yes, I know god very well. He must be very fond of me, too, making me remember him so much.'

'Does he know me, Mother?' asked Jatila curiously. 'I should like to know him, too.'

'You'll know one day whether you want to know him or not, and if he wants to know you,' said his mother, getting up to go inside, and no more conversations were had about god.

Jatila tried very hard to be brave the next day when he walked home from school but the growl of some wild beast in the bushes when he was midway in the forest frightened him badly. He tore home again, collapsing in tears at his mother's feet.

'Mother, I don't want to go to school any more. The forest frightens me too much, even in the morning, sometimes,' he wept.

His mother bit her lip and looked away. Jatila saw that she was looking hard at the prayer corner where an oil lamp was lit every evening at the feet of the family idols. She seemed to be thinking something over.

She gave a little nod suddenly and turned to look at Jatila again.

'I didn't remember Madhusudan,' she said with a rueful smile. 'Come here; let me dry your face. The next time you're afraid, just call out to Madhusudan. He'll look after you.'

'Who is he, Mother?' asked Jatila.

'He's your elder brother,' said his mother, laughing, but nicely now.

Jatila was very excited. 'Why didn't you tell me I had a big brother? Why does he never come home? What does he look like?' he asked.

'He likes to live in the forest, so I haven't seen him for a long time,' said his mother. 'He's tall and dark and quite strong. Perhaps he'll come home one day though right now he seems very far away.'

Jatila could hardly sleep that night thinking of his big brother. Wait till he told the boys at school, he thought, it was a fine thing to boast of, to have an elder brother.

Full of these happy plans, he was very disappointed the next morning when his mother told him just as he was leaving for school, 'You mustn't tell anybody about Madhusudan. He may never want to meet you if you talk about him at school or in the village. You can talk about him to me, of course.'

'I won't, I promise,' said Jatila in a small voice and trudged off bravely into the forest, which had begun to get slightly more familiar each day.

It seemed as though Jatila was finally getting over his fear of the forest when one day just before school closed for the monsoon during the four months of chaturmaas, a big storm blew over the forest. The sky grew dark and the forest even darker in the early thunderstorm. The wind whipped through the trees, which creaked and groaned alarmingly, and dust, leaves and even twigs hit Jatila in the face as he tried to walk as fast as he could, afraid to run in the blinding storm.

A broken branch fell across the narrow jungle path suddenly, barely missing Jatila, and he felt more afraid than ever. And then he remembered his elder brother.

'Brother Madhusudan!' he called as loudly as he could above the storm.

But there was no answer, only the wicked wheeze and whirl of the forest creaking around Jatila.

Jatila called and called until he was hoarse, growing more and more afraid.

'Come to me, I'm afraid. Where are you, brother?' He began to weep aloud.

'Don't be afraid, here I am,' said a calm, strong voice behind him all at once. Jatila spun around but saw no one.

'I can't see you!' he cried pitifully. 'Please come to me, Brother Madhusudan.'

'Keep walking, Jatila, I'm watching your back. Keep walking, don't be afraid,' said the voice.

Feeling comforted, Jatila began to walk on boldly. The storm died away after a while and he found himself at the edge of the forest.

'Now, let me see you!' he cried and whirled around. But there was nobody on the path. Jatila heard a laugh close by from behind the trees.

'I could not keep away when you called, Jatila,' he heard the voice say. 'I'll take you through whenever you need me. Don't be afraid, lion-heart. You're very, very brave. You just didn't know it. But you do now.'

Jatila called out a fond goodbye and ran home to tell his mother. It was wonderful to know that he had someone of his own to take him through the forest.

Perhaps Madhusudan would appear one day, after all? It was something to look forward to now, every day.

18

The Mistake

Ramana Maharishi (1879–1950) was only sixteen when he had a mystic near-death experience that he described as 'a great flame'. Born into a devotional milieu in the old Madras Presidency, he interpreted it as a spiritual union with Shiva. It was powerful enough to make him leave home a few weeks later to live as a sanyasi for the rest of his life on Arunachala Hill, an ancient site of Shaiva pilgrimage. His gentle mystical air attracted many devotees and inquiring Englishmen like Raphael Hurst, also known as 'Paul Brunton', author of *A Search in Secret India*, made him known in the West in the 1930s. Ramana Maharishi took a conciliatory view of various religious paths and practices and personally recommended independent reasoning as a sound approach to spiritual awareness. He also upheld bhakti or emotional surrender – ideally to the impersonal 'self' identified as 'god' by Upanishadic thinkers. It was a modern combination of clinical ancient philosophy and unquestioning medieval devotion. Once, a devotee who had lost his only son came grieving to Ramana Maharishi who reportedly consoled him with the key points of this parable from the *Vichara Sagara* by Nischal Dasji (1791–1863), a Dadupanthi sadhu whose Hindi interpretation of the Upanishads in this book was immensely popular as daily reading across the North.

Rama and Krishna grew up together in the same small town deep in the Hindi heartland. Their families were friends and had lived next to each other in ancestral houses for generations. The boys were the only sons of their parents and petted and spoiled by everybody in the food chain from grandfathers and great-uncles down to all the women and girls and all the servants too.

When they were sent to the paathshala or local school, they set off together and came back together. When they set foot into their respective havelis, they did exactly the same thing. They sat down on a carved and cushioned chair and held out their feet. A servant would take off their shoes, wash their feet in a basin and dry them. They could now go into the inner rooms, leaving their footwear to be dusted, wiped and put away by the servant.

The moment the boys stepped inside the inner rooms, their mothers would spring up and hug them in welcome. As if in mirror image, each boy was made to do exactly the same thing in his house. He would sit down on a low wooden seat and his hands would be washed and dried. His sisters would run to fetch him a thaali with fresh, hot rotis and many bowls of delicious food on the great brass plate and Rama and Krishna would eat their luxurious fill as if they were indeed the King of Ayodhya and the King of Dwarka respectively.

A short nap followed lunch or maybe a game of pachisi with their sisters while the rest of the household dozed. The boys ran out to play at four o'clock, to fly kites, run races, climb trees or swim in the baoli, the big stepwell that no boy could resist. It was like a swimming pool with high steps above the water on all sides. The boys were expert divers though their mothers repeatedly begged them not to risk cracking their skulls on the sandstone steps.

This idyll ended when they turned sixteen. They had learned Persian and Arabic in addition to Hindi and a smattering of Sanskrit, and served out their apprenticeship with local jewellers. They now made a plan to go to Surat for more experience with the gemstone experts there and after a year take ship to Basra to become traders in seed pearls for the jewellery market of Jaipur. Their families wept but did not oppose their darlings in their adventurous plans on the condition that they come home in two years to be married on Akha Teej day.

Everything went as planned and Rama and Krishna had a high old time in Basra. They were good-looking, well-grown, well-schooled young men and their Indian contacts in Basra took them home, where they soon became the darlings of those families and were pampered almost as if they had never left home at all.

They made secret plans to marry the daughters of their Indian patrons in Basra and never go back. Who would console their families back home, though? With typical youthful insouciance they decided to deal with the situation when it arose and carried on enjoying themselves at work and play. They made a few good friends among the local young men and were soon to be seen riding and camping in the wadis with them. They began to make plans to visit the fabled city of Damascus in Syria, stirred by travellers' tales of picnics in the orchards of the Ghuta, the cool, sweet water of the Fija springs and mountain holidays in Baladoun. And really, how could they not visit Isfahan in Iran and buy fine silk carpets for their lodgings?

Rama and Krishna made good money now and began to eye houses in Basra. They wanted to live next to each other as they had at home. But one fateful day, Rama caught an infection in the bazaar. His sores spread all over his body and neither the costliest treatment nor the most expensive hakim was able to save him. Krishna had to cremate Rama with a heavy heart. His local friends doubled their pampering in an effort to console him and soon Krishna was married exactly as planned; he also bought a grand house and became a prosperous merchant. All this took a mere five years and in all this while there was no news of the families in India nor had the boys sent word, always intending to but not finding anyone who was able to to make the journey inland to their home town from Surat port.

At last, Krishna met an Indian merchant who would pass close by his home and persuaded him to make the detour to personally inform his parents that he was doing very well, had settled down with a wife in a fine big house and even had a little son of his own. The merchant was also charged with the sad task of informing Rama's parents of his death.

However, it took the merchant several months to get to Rama and Krishna's home town. He decided to get over with the sad news first. But by mistake, instead of going to Rama's house, he went to Krishna's and gravely informed his family that he was the bearer of bad news. Their son Krishna had died of a fever in Basra. He spared them the details of the bazaar infection and the sores all over his body. Shrieks of sorrow rent the air in Krishna's house and the merchant excused himself and hurried next door, where he told Rama's parents that their son was doing very well indeed and had a wife and son. He was sorry he had forgotten their names, but the wife was an Indian girl. He handed Krishna's presents for his family to Rama's. Rama's father was thrilled with the heavy gold kara and his mother was delighted with the dainty satlada or seven-stringed necklace of gems that her son had thoughtfully sent her and the hooped golden earrings with clusters of fine Basra pearls for the girls, who were now married and gone.

While Rama's family rejoiced, Krishna's family grieved inconsolably for their dead son. The facts were different but to them, perception was reality. Neither family thought to send a representative to Basra or go themselves to verify the matter. They lived by what they were told and never considered the deeper reality that their sons had actually left them years ago. It did not really matter if they were dead or alive for Rama and Krishna had long ceased to be physical presences to their families. The boys lived only in their hearts as dear memories to which the families remained attached.

It was nearly a year before Krishna's messenger returned to Basra and it was only when Krishna questioned him that he realized his terrible mistake. He was ashamed and extremely apologetic and offered to go back to set matters right on his next trip the following year. But upon reflection, Krishna told him not to. It would be cruel to Rama's parents and his own family already mourned him as dead.

'Best let it be,' thought Krishna practically and was never heard of again in his home town where his parents ritually sent up prayers for his soul every year for the next ten years until they passed away, while Rama's parents wondered why he never came home or sent word for the rest of their lives.

19

Value for Money

Swami Sivananda (1887–1963) was born in Tirunelveli and excelled in his youth at studies and as a gymnast. He served for some years as a physician in British Malaya and came home in 1923, impelled to go on a spiritual journey. He visited holy places like Varanasi and Nashik before he took sanyas in 1924 and went to live at Muni ki Reti in Rishikesh on the Ganga, where he spent most of his life. Immersing himself in spiritual practices, he also began to actively serve the poor. When the insurance policy from his former worldly life matured, he used the money to found a free dispensary at the perennially crowded pilgrim site of Lakshman Jhula at Haridwar where he personally attended to the ailing. The swami later went on an all-India pilgrimage and sang and danced in spiritual ecstasy at Ramana Maharishi's ashram, as Sri Chaitanya Mahaprabhu once did in Nabadwip and Vrindavan. Swami Sivananda founded the Divine Life Society in 1936 to promote awareness of spirituality and culture, which attracted many followers and became an international movement for yoga and social service. He authored over 200 books on yoga, Vedanta, the lives of saints and related subjects. A brief parable attributed to him is expanded and retold to portray the values he stood for.

Vidya Bhushan had two sons named Vishal and Vivek. His wife was dead and he had to bring up his boys as a single parent. His old mother lived with them and generally saw to things but to spare her, Vidya Bhushan did most of the cooking himself before he took his sons to school and went to work. Luckily, his job as a clerk in the municipal corporation had regular hours and weekends off. Vidya Bhushan used his evenings and holidays well, helping his boys with their homework, teaching them their prayers and getting his mother to tell them interesting stories from the epics and the lives of saints. He took the boys on brief visits to the temple on Mondays and encouraged them to be outdoors as much as possible during daylight.

'You must run and play and grow strong,' he said and never grudged the expense if the boys wanted a new ball or even a cricket bat for their afternoon games in the maidan with their friends. He especially liked to take the boys to the local orphanage on Sunday mornings, where his colleague at the municipal corporation took free bhajan classes once a week for the younger children. Vidya Bhushan volunteered at the orphanage himself on Sunday mornings to help the older boys in language and mathematics. During that time, his sons were allowed to join the bhajan class and learned to sing the cheerful devotional songs chosen by the colleague, who had his own theories on character-building.

'It's too easy to preach and say do this, do that,' he'd say as he walked home with Vidya Bhushan and his sons. 'These poor boys are wretched enough already with no one of their own. The only thing we can give them is a bit of cheer and something to hold on to, that not only do they have friends outside but also that each one of them has a Friend within. The songs I like to teach them are not about the sorrows of life but about getting to know the Friend within.'

'And how may anyone find that Friend within?' asked Vidya Bhushan, nudging his boys to listen attentively.

'Only if we make an effort to be friends with the people we meet in everyday life,' said the colleague.

'But not everyone is friendly. Some people like to cheat others,' said Vidya Bhushan.

'Well, why did god give us wit? We must think for ourselves a bit, too,' laughed the colleague.

Satisfied with this answer, Vidya Bhushan invited his friend home to lunch the next Sunday after class at the orphanage.

'Do you have a favourite dish? I cook for my family and I will try to make it for you,' he said when the colleague smilingly accepted the invitation.

'Thank you! Now let me see...I like most things and wouldn't like to give you trouble,' said the colleague.

'No, do tell me.'

'Well, since you ask, I'm very partial to brinjals and potatoes in thick tomato gravy with hot ajwain parathas and cucumber raita,' said the colleague. 'It's one of my favourite combinations but my wife and mother are away to attend a wedding and mean to make a long visit. The boy who helps out in their absence is an indifferent cook, so I rather miss it.'

'Oh, we can feed you that; it's a pleasure,' said Vidya Bhushan and they parted on the best of terms, greatly pleased with their small, delightful plans.

Vidya Bhushan was greatly struck by the colleague's point on everyone having to use their share of wit. He often wondered if he was bringing up his sons well single-handed, and he now thought of a way to test them to find out. Vishal was ten and Vivek was eleven years old and he could not make out from their everyday behaviour if they were growing up right, for they were both moderately good at their studies and were just normal children otherwise.

Next Saturday, he summoned his sons late in the afternoon.

'My colleague is coming to lunch tomorrow as you know, so we won't be going to our usual Sunday class,' he told them. 'Here's ten rupees each. Please go to the market and fetch me some brinjals for tomorrow's lunch. I'm sending you both to look since I promised him brinjal curry. You can keep the change and spend it as you like.'

Pleased and proud to be asked, the little boys set off at once for the market and agreed to look at two opposite ends. Vishal went up to the very first vegetable seller he saw and held out the ten-rupee note.

'Please give me ten brinjals for this – my father wants to make a good curry,' he said.

The vegetable seller knew at once that a simpleton stood before him. He gave him ten rotten brinjals from a heap of wormy ones that he had just culled and kept aside. With his errand and money both out of the way, Vishal wandered around the market happily looking at everything.

Meanwhile Vivek took a good look around him at two or three vegetable stalls and finally stopped at the one where he saw a glistening heap of fresh brinjals, their whole, perfect skins gleaming silky purple.

'I'd like a kilo of those at your best rate and please give me the exact change,' he said politely but confidently. It cost him four annas, a mere quarter of a rupee. Bearing away this booty, Vivek came to a halt by a temple to Ganesha. 'It's my first pocket money, I should offer some to god in thanks before I spend it,' he thought. He bought a few bananas for two rupees that he offered in puja, and received some of it back as consecrated food, along with a few flowers and a small paper packet of holy ash. He put away the prasad to take home to his family.

'But it's not really enough in offering, I haven't given anything to people,' he thought and counted out another five rupees that he gave away to the beggar children sitting in a line near the shrine. They smiled sunnily up at him and chirped the beggar's blessings they had been taught in their clear, childish voices.

Vivek stopped for a look next at the shrine's little

kiosk where he spotted small booklets of stories about the gods, and spent the rest of his money buying a few to take home to share.

Vishal and Vivek arrived home within minutes of each other to find Vidya Bhushan waiting for them.

'Look, Father, ten brinjals for ten rupees; they ought to be wonderful,' said Vishal and produced the ten rotten brinjals.

Vidya Bhushan's heart sank. He could tell at once that the brinjals were no good. Ten rotten brinjals? For ten whole rupees?

'I see,' he said quietly and turned to Vivek. 'And what have you brought?' he asked.

Vivek laid out his shopping.

'Prasad for you all, Father,' he said cheerfully. 'The brinjals look good, don't they? They cost four annas. I gave five rupees away to the beggar children, you know. You did say we could spend the change as we pleased, didn't you, Father?'

'What made you do that?' asked Vidya Bhushan, deeply interested in the reason for this philanthropy.

'Father, I know we're going to have a very good lunch tomorrow and probably a nice dinner tonight as well. We eat well every day, don't we? So I wanted them to have something, too, because they don't…' Vivek faltered, suddenly wondering if he had done the wrong thing.

'It's all right. You did well. And what else did you buy?'

'See these storybooks from the temple, Father? We don't have these at home. I thought we'd all read them, Granny, too,' said Vivek.

Vidya Bhushan felt his eyes mist over. An image of his dead wife came to him. Just so had she liked to give things away to people and get things for them in small, sweet gestures of loving kindness.

Vivek would be all right, he thought in relief. The boy had thought his way through this small but important responsibility and had not only shopped correctly but also spent his money with good thoughts on good things.

How was he going to make Vishal understand, though?

'Well, he's only ten, after all,' Vidya Bhushan consoled himself, as the boys went in to show their grandmother the storybooks and give her a share of the prasad. 'I have many years to work on him yet, I hope. I'll ask my colleague his advice, too, on how I can make Vishal more aware of himself and the world.'

He gathered up the brinjals and made his way to the kitchen, mentally reviewing the recipe for lunch the next day.

20

A Drink of Water

This tale, once told with variations by grandmothers from a previous century in South India, was also retold by the late Sathya Sai Baba (1926–2011). He was born in Puttaparthi in what is now Andhra Pradesh and was reportedly stung by a scorpion when he was fourteen. The legend goes that he lost consciousness for several days and when he recovered, his behaviour changed dramatically, with long silences, bouts of weeping and the sudden ability to sing in Sanskrit. He attracted a huge following at home and in the world and built ashrams, schools, colleges and hospitals. He was given a massive state funeral attended by the Indian prime minister and senior political leaders; and the Dalai Lama and the Sri Lankan president sent condolences.

This concluding parable once told by him brings us back to the Upanishadic message 'Datta. Give, be generous' of the first story in this collection, 'What the Thunder Says'. It is set in Varanasi or Kashi, the world's oldest living city that has operated for millennia as 'Hindu Central' in the subcontinent's grid of sacred geography and it upholds the core credo repeated by gurus, reformers and iconoclasts across epochs and regions that it's 'humanity first', not dry ritual.

Charandas was the laziest young man in his obscure village, always looking for a shortcut. His father had been the village shopkeeper but a sudden fire had destroyed the little wooden kiosk and his father, having lost his livelihood, had died of shock. Charandas's mother was long dead. He was loosely adopted by the village and had managed to evade his lessons and learning a trade or skill. He had no capital to set up shop with, no uncles to be apprenticed to, and was too indolent to go seek his fortune elsewhere. Instead, he appeared every day at various homes with a big grin and rubbed his belly significantly. He knew perfectly well that the villagers would give him something to eat just to make him go away. Finally the village council decided that he had become a liability and had to do some work, for which he could then be paid and thereby live off his earnings instead of being a menace to society, especially at lunchtime.

Accordingly, he was sent to drive the village buffaloes to the river and bring them back safely by the afternoon in time for milking, which task suited his idle nature perfectly. Charandas lived in a mud hut on the edge of his village and only bathed 'from Deepavali to Deepavali' as the saying went, his habits being wholly irregular.

One day, the village buzzed with excitement. The priest at their local Shiva temple had come back safely from a long pilgrimage and in thanksgiving had exchanged the copper pot above the shivling for a silver one. Water dripped from a fine hole in the pot to 'cool' the fiery cosmic energy of Shiva symbolized by the shivling. It was a beautiful sight. Even Charandas was roused to drop by for a look, spurred by all the talk.

'Where did you buy this fine silver pot?' asked the villagers and the priest said, 'At Kashi, of course. You can get everything fine there, be it in copper, silver or gold, and the grandest cloth fit for kings.'

'Ah, everyone must go there once, it's our religious duty,' said the villagers and noted with satisfaction that their priest had also replenished the temple's supply of Ganga water from Kashi with a big sealed copper pot. No temple anywhere in the land was properly consecrated without the presence of holy Ganga water from Kashi's sacred ghats and anybody about to die was given a sip. Ganga water never grew stale, that was its unique property; it was the purest water in the world. People from the most remote and rugged hamlets thousands of miles away who made the long, hard pilgrimage to Kashi always took home these sealed pots of Ganga water. This renewed their link with the holiest of holy cities; indeed, they did not dare go home without it.

Charandas looked doubtfully at the silver pot. He really could not see what the fuss was about.

'Ah, you have done our village a real service with this fine offering,' he heard someone say. 'You must have spent all your savings on it. A man may sell this pot and stay home doing nothing for a year at least.'

Gawping at the pot from behind the others, Charandas felt as though lightning had hit his body.

'I must have that pot,' he thought. 'I will go to Kashi, sell it and live easy for a whole year. And when the money's over, I'm sure I'll find something else to steal. If it's such a big, rich place, I'll never be found out.'

His fall from grace was as simple as that. The years of laziness had filled him up with the sludge of tamas, of negative energy. All it took was one tempting possibility to push him over. Charandas ran away with the silver pot that very night. He made his way to Kashi by a circuitous route, cajoling rides on sugarcane carts and vegetable carts and walking when he had to.

When he got to Kashi, it was the work of minutes to sell the silver pot and find a place to stay not far from Harischandra Ghat where the most funerals were held. It was said that the fires on this ghat had not gone out for 5000 years but Charandas did not care; he was there to observe the mourners. When he saw wealthy mourners leave the ghat after consigning their dead ones to the flames, he followed them discreetly to their homes or lodging and was usually able to relieve them of money or jewellery and sometimes both. It required a fair amount of work but Charandas did not see it as that. It seemed the most marvellous shortcut to him to be a thief and live 'for free'. Several years passed in this manner.

Meanwhile, one day from up on Mount Kailash, the goddess Parvati cast an anxious eye on Kashi.

'Shiva, my lord, do look below at how the place teems with people,' she said. 'Everyone comes there to pay their respects to you as Lord of the World at Kashi and each one believes they will escape rebirth because of that and come straight here to us. Do we even have place on Kailash for so many souls?'

Shiva was very amused. 'Don't worry, that won't happen,' he laughed. 'Most of them will never make it. Shall we go see how it works? What do you say to a bit of drama? We'll go in disguise to Kashi.'

Parvati agreed happily and the father and the mother of the universe took their place at the entrance to the alley that led to Kashi Vishwanath's temple. Parvati was disguised as a weak old lady in rags and Shiva, equally ragged and emaciated, lay curled up on the ground beside her disguised as a pathetic old man.

Hundreds of freshly bathed, well-dressed worshippers went busily past this derelict pair, each carefully carrying a pot of Ganga water to pour in offering on the great shivling in the temple.

But they were deaf to the moans of the old man and indifferent to the cries of the old lady who begged them to please give her husband a drink of water. Not one person stopped for them. They were carrying holy water to make an offering to god for their own salvation and did not mean to waste it on dirty old beggars. Passing uncaringly by the father and the mother of the universe, they hurried to pour water on a stone.

By and by, Charandas strolled up to the temple. It was

a Monday, the day of the week dedicated to Shiva, and the crowd was double as always. He made a good haul on Mondays at Kashi Vishwanath's door, picking pockets and bags in the throng.

Intent on spotting victims, he tripped unseeingly over the old beggars and fell to the ground. The old man groaned horribly in pain but the old lady with him, instead of scolding Charandas, asked him anxiously if he had hurt himself.

'No, Granny, I'm all right,' said Charandas, touched by this unexpected concern.

'Please, my boy, fetch my husband a sip of holy water. He is almost dead and there is no one willing to give him that absolution,' begged the old lady piteously.

Charandas took out the hollowed toria gourd that served as his water bottle, glad he had just refilled it with the holy water that flowed so plentifully by. He unplugged the gourd and leaned towards the old man.

'Please speak a word of truth in his ear, child,' said the old lady softly.

'I don't get your meaning, Granny,' said Charandas, surprised.

'My husband is on the point of death. He's holding on somehow until a drop of holy water wets his throat. Please whisper in his ear about a good deed you've done while you pour water into his mouth,' urged the old lady.

Charandas winced in sudden shame.

'Granny,' he said awkwardly, 'I'm a thief! I can't think of a single good thing I've done in my whole life. The truth is that this is my very first good deed,' and he carefully poured a little water into the old man's mouth.

The beggars disappeared in the blink of an eye and in their place stood Shiva and Parvati, glowing in utter beauty as Gauri–Shankar, the divine couple. Only Charandas could see them and was stunned by their radiance. He stared with his mouth open before scrambling to fall in salute. 'My mother, my father,' he wept as he touched the dust at their feet. 'Forgive me. I am unworthy.'

'Do get up,' he heard the lord say in a kind voice. 'You have wiped out your lazy, thieving past by taking pity on a wretched old pair of beggars. We bless you for it.'

The heavenly vision faded and Charandas made his way back in a happy uplifted state to his lodgings. It felt very good to know that he was capable of a good deed and he wanted to hold on to that feeling. His mind felt cleansed of negative energy. Instead, he now felt charged with good purpose and considered what to do next. First things first, he decided, and counted his money. There was enough to buy a new silver pot in place of the one he had stolen and enough to go home. He would offer himself in the temple's service as atonement. He would beg the priest to teach him the lessons he had avoided in the village school and think of what to do with his life after that.

~

Back on Kailash, Shiva and Parvati looked down compassionately on the world.

'Poor things,' said Parvati with motherly pity. 'I do hate to see them suffer.'

'They don't realize that they're in charge of their salvation, not us,' said Shiva. 'But when they do, it's a short step home to Kailash.'

A Note on the Author

Renuka Narayanan writes on religion and culture. She was the religion editor of the *Hindustan Times* for many years.

Click the QR Code with a QR scanner app or type the link into the Internet browser on your phone to download the app.